HIDDEN HISTORY *of* BARRE, VERMONT

HIDDEN HISTORY *of* BARRE, VERMONT

RUSSELL J. BELDING

THE History PRESS

Published by The History Press
Charleston, SC 29403
www.historypress.net

First published 2011

Manufactured in the United States

ISBN 978.1.60949.092.8

Library of Congress Cataloging-in-Publication Data

Hidden history of Barre, Vermont / [compiled by] Russell Belding.
p. cm.
ISBN 978-1-60949-092-8
1. Barre (Vt.)--History. 2. Barre (Vt.)--Biography. 3. Barre (Vt.)--Social life and customs. 4. American newspapers--Vermont--Barre. 5. Gossip columns--Vermont--Barre. I. Belding, Russell.
F59.B17H53 2011
974.3'4--dc22
2011010587

Notice: The information in this book is true and complete to the best of our knowledge. It is offered without guarantee on the part of the author or The History Press. The author and The History Press disclaim all liability in connection with the use of this book.

Contents

Introduction 7

1. "Barre Bundle": 1874–97 11
2. "Talk of the Town" and "Sparks of Granite City": 1897–1910 27
3. Local News Ascendant: 1911–27 47
4. After the Flood and Through the War: 1927–45 75
5. After the War: 1946 60 99
6. Slow Fade-Out: 1960–70 115

Afterword 125
About the Author 127

Introduction

This book is an anthology of typical and/or interesting submissions from local newspaper correspondents working in Barre, Vermont, over the course of about a century.

Our story begins in 1863, when Hiram Atkins founded the Montpelier *Argus & Patriot*, a weekly newspaper that seems to have had a degree of statewide circulation. In any case, before his paper was many years old, Atkins was including local ephemera under headings such as "Williamstown Whispers," "Pawlet Ponderings" and "Montpelier Mere Mention." Items in these sections, which came from most corners of the state, would run from ten to a couple of hundred words and told of important events, the doings of prominent individuals, comings and goings, births and deaths or anything that seemed gossip worthy. The Barre column, initially called "Barre Bits," acquired the name "Barre Bundle" around 1875. In 1897, Atkins supplemented his weekly with the daily Montpelier *Evening Argus*. The weekly folded not long afterward.

Barre itself, meanwhile, had a weekly known as the *Granite City Leader*. This paper was run by John W. Ramsey and Clayton J. Kinsley for most of its existence, although Mr. Ramsey died in 1895. The *Leader* published from 1892 through 1897. Ramsey and Kinsley were not as ambitious as Atkins regarding local correspondents, keeping a smaller stable of them. The *Leader* was more of a hometown paper than the *Argus & Patriot*.

Frank Langley arrived in Barre early in 1897, having previously been located in Gloversville, New York, where a daily newspaper under his proprietorship had gone under a few months before. Langley managed to make a success of the *Barre Daily Times*, beginning on March 16. From the first issue until several months after the paper merged with the Montpelier *Evening Argus* sixty-two years later, every day's paper contained a local correspondent's column, known as "Talk of the Town." Unlike Atkins's "Barre Bundle," which tended to be outspoken about various subjects, especially those of a political nature, the *Times*'s editor, Dean H. Perry, exercised more caution as to whose feathers the paper ruffled. But if there was less controversy, there was no lack of entertainment for the reader. At least until the late 1920s, there was a consistent authorial voice that the loyal reader of "Talk of the Town" could recognize, and rumor has it that that voice belonged to Perry. In addition, as the years progressed, most Vermont towns within thirty miles of Barre, and some beyond that distance, had their own regular *Barre Times* correspondent, some of them quite loquacious. The number of correspondents probably reached a peak sometime in the 1920s. But somehow they were seldom as lively as "Talk of the Town."

About a year after the *Times*'s debut, the *Barre Evening Enterprise* made its first appearance on the city's streets. With the advent of the Spanish-American War, the *Enterprise* provided a second option for a news-hungry public. The paper's name soon changed to the *Barre Evening Telegram*. For much of its existence, the *Telegram* was more of a scandal sheet than the staid *Times*, although its local column, "Sparks from Granite City," was fairly similar to that of its rival, albeit with more typographical errors. After a brief tenure as a morning paper, the *Telegram* ceased publication in 1905.

As noted above, the *Times* continued with "Talk of the Town" for the length of the paper's existence. In 1959, the owner of the *Times* purchased the *Montpelier Evening Argus*. Thus was born the *Times-Argus*, which continues (minus the hyphen) to this day. As the *Times-Argus* ostensibly represented both cities, "Talk of the Town" was retired in early June 1960 and replaced by "Barre News Notes." Similarly, the *Argus*'s "News of the City" column became "Capital News Notes." Compared with the columns of thirty or forty years before, "Barre News Notes" was mostly made up of tersely told facts, eliminating the amusing anecdotes.

"Barre News Notes" suffered a slow death, still making isolated appearances in occasional issues of the *Times Argus* as late as 1985. Almost all of the local correspondents had long since disappeared, however.

This author has chosen to feature columns from the *Argus & Patriot*, the *Barre Daily Times*, the *Barre Evening Telegram* and the *Times-Argus*, using the period from 1875 to 1970. The book features a combination of unusually interesting items and fairly typical ones. The reader perhaps may notice a change both in subject matter and writing styles as the years progress.

If history in the past has mostly focused on the great doings of great people, the current definition of the word—especially in the "local history" sphere—can be said to possess a greater inclusiveness of the ordinary doings of ordinary people. While this seems laudable, it should be noted that, if more things constitute history, and the size of books does not accordingly expand, a greater proportion of relevant material will be left out. To put it still another way, the editors of the newspapers quoted throughout this book used their own biases, the papers' deadline and the biases of their correspondents to decide what would get into the paper. I, in turn, used my own judgment many years later to decide which proportionally tiny handful of the hundreds of thousands of items should be included here. It would be a lie to say that I have read every one of those many items, but I have at least run my eyes over every column, searching some of the tastier Barre Bits.

In a couple of cases ("drouth" for "drought" and "employe" for "employee"), the arcane spelling has been retained as it appeared in the original newspaper column.

Chapter 1

"Barre Bundle"

1874–97

Much of the purpose of the *Argus & Patriot*'s many local columns was to provide hometown information to people who had moved out of town or out of state. Thus, the "Barre Bundle" included not only ephemeral items but news of some importance. The latter, however, will not be highlighted here.

This was the period of Barre's most intense growth. The branch of the Central Vermont Railroad reached town in 1875, and another branch reached up the hill to the granite quarries in 1888. What had been a fairly typical northern New England farming community was suddenly faced with an influx of immigrants from Scotland and Italy, along with (somewhat later) Spain, French Canada and other faraway places, all coming to make their living by either quarrying or carving stone or by employing others to quarry or carve stone. Barre Village was incorporated in 1887, and in 1894, a bill was sent to the state legislature, changing Barre Village into Barre City, separating it from the rest of the town.

While looking at all this with some bemusement, the *Argus & Patriot*'s correspondent, or "the Bundler" as he called himself, still treated the city as if it was a small town with the usual small-town foibles (which, in the larger scheme of things, it probably was).

At times, the Bundler could be terse for comic effect. At other times, the brevity seems oddly misplaced to modern eyes. And, at still other times,

Barre before the granite boom, early 1870s, looking toward the village common. The town hall is to the left. *Vermont Historical Society.*

the news is so inconsequential that one wonders how readers of the time would have cared. Herein, some random samples of brevity:

January 21, 1875: "Ira Howland was kicked by a goat Saturday of last week, breaking his collar bone."

February 18, 1880: "The strike at the Fork Factory last week lasted about thirty minutes, or until Freeman Holden told the strikers that they could have their choice, go to work at the old rates, or leave the shop."

October 6, 1880: "George Bishop lost a $10 bill, last Friday night, between Twingsville and the post-office."

May 13, 1885: "Nearly all of the shade trees set last year have succumbed to the drouth of last summer, or some other causes."

February 26, 1890: "The amiable dog of William Quinn last Sunday reduced the dog of George C. Mackie to mince-meat, and Mr. Mackie is naturally indignant."

September 23, 1891: "Lightning struck the porch of the residence of Crawford Jackson last Thursday night, tearing off the paper with which it was covered."

April 6, 1892: "A crippled wheel of a buggy in which A.A. Skinner was riding last Friday dumped that gentleman in the mud and very unceremoniously, but fortunately not injuring him."

January 16, 1895: "John Calgin was arrested last week for selling Jamaica ginger by Officer Hutchinson, and was sentenced to Rutland for 90 days."

Some items seemed calculated to warn certain unnamed parties (via broad hints) that exposure would soon follow if their bad behavior continued. This type of item might be summed up as "I'm not one to gossip, so I won't mention any names, but…" Some examples follow:

November 29, 1876: "The good people of Barre were disgusted at the musical talent of the serenaders last Wednesday and Thursday nights, the tumult of tin pans, horns and cow-bells making the night hideous."

November 13, 1878: "Three young South Barre chaps returned from the Capital on Saturday evening, sufficiently etherized to make themselves a nuisance in the cars. Passing up street, they waylaid belligerently several persons. On their way home they stopped Widow Waterman's carriage, in which her son and daughter were riding, seizing the horse's bridle. Miss Waterman told them to let go, as she knew them. Her brother struck the horse, knocking down one fellow, when the wheel went over him. They then went on to Cold Spring, met Wilbur Shepherd, and stopped his horse. He drove them off. On Sunday they went and apologized to the Waterman's, saying they were drunk, and meant no harm. But such kind of drunken frolics should not be tolerated. If legally investigated, the young men's names would of course legitimately come before the public."

August 13, 1879: "There were one or more 'howlers' around last Saturday night, who used the meetinghouse sheds for lodgings. Stay at home next time, and avoid trouble."

January 11, 1882: "A female denizen of Barre has been visiting Montpelier quite frequently of late, and it is rumored that some of 'the boys' have formed her acquaintance to their sorrow. She is said to be a 'lovely' character."

March 29, 1882: "E.W. Bisbee rushed up stairs to his office one evening recently, and on opening the entry door was nearly knocked

Barre Universalist Church, shortly after major alterations, circa 1877. *Vermont Historical Society.*

over by a female, who was making a hasty exit. 'Ed' started to investigate, when a man shot through the door into outer darkness, both going so quickly he could not see who they were. Now Bisbee wants to know what they wanted."

May 9, 1883: "Would it not be well for even ladies to ask permission before entering private grounds to dig vegetables? It would save them some notification at least."

October 15, 1884: "There is one husband at least in town who need have no fears in leaving his wife alone over night, as she is sure of male protection in such an event."

January 21, 1885: "A young gentleman has been paying his attentions to a lady in a neighboring town; now her parents are anxious that the marriage ceremony should be performed before many weeks pass."

June 17, 1885: "Would it not be well for a certain married man and that young lady from Orange, to be a little more careful when they are both occupying one chair to have the curtain down, so that that young man, passing through his door yard, will not see what is going on? Or would it not be better still, if the mother cares anything for the reputation of her child, to take her home and try and save her? All lovers of first class scandal will have their fill of this matter soon. Perhaps some other

Goddard Seminary, not long after its 1870 opening. This was on the present site of Barre's Municipal Auditorium. *Aldrich Library Collection.*

peculiar circumstances may be all right, but a cloak of religion does not always cover up defects."

November 2, 1887: "The services of the public are needed to suppress a male nuisance, who has for several evenings past by lighting friction matches attracted attention from chamber windows while he made an indecent exposure of his person. The fellow was captured a few nights since, begged off, and offered to pay; but his money was refused. But the very next night he, or some one of his kind, repeated the beastly offense. Respectable people do not like to prosecute such skunks, and the only way to get the law on them is for the police to make an arrest."

November 28, 1888: "Some time last summer a young lady living at the quarries brought into this world a fine boy baby, the only trouble with the infant being the cloud that obscured its parentage on the other side. She apparently regretted this deviation from the course of virtue, and last week united herself in marriage with a gentleman in her neighborhood. Her father was much more incensed at this lawful act then he was at the unlawful caper which she previously cut, and took, as rumor goes, a very curious method of showing his displeasure. For fear his family might derive any benefit from a fine orchard which he possessed, he cut down all the trees in it, and burned the remains. Having thus eased his mind, he proceeded to let nature take its course."

May 1, 1889: "There is a nuisance in Barre that is even worse than its vicious dogs, and that is the wretched youths who make a practice of going about at night and wantonly breaking windows with slingshots. Several church windows have been smashed, and any number in private residences. It is hard to account for such youthful depravity, but if several enraged citizens can catch a few of these malicious youngsters a good deal of the depravity will be taken out with a horsewhip."

July 10, 1889: "The young lady in the South Main street boarding house should 'roll down the blinds,' especially when not in her own room."

January 13, 1892: "Because a deputy sheriff is efficacious in enforcing the prohibitory law, does that give him the right to get drunk himself?"

May 22, 1895: "The midnight brawls in certain houses in the lower end of town are getting to be disgraceful. Last Saturday night several heads were smashed open with beer bottles and some one will soon be waking up behind the golden gates if matters are allowed to progress as they have been going."

Similarly, the Bundler would at times have fun with certain residents who had gotten into embarrassing situations:

July 3, 1878: "Charles L. Williams, aged 30 years, came to an untimely end financially last week Tuesday. For several years he has been a successful carriage maker in town, and everybody supposed him to be an honest young man. His sudden departure caused a large interested circle to mourn. His demise was similar to that which took off his late friend, E.O. Leonard. Pleasant and smiling in their lives, in their departure they were not long divided. It is hoped they will meet in some happier clime, where men may borrow always, and never be obliged to pay. The only mourning one who smiles through his tears is J.H. Jones, who, when asked about his claim, smiles serenely, and whispers, 'secured.' Requiescat in pace."

March 26, 1879: "Mr. A.C. Shepard, residing in the south part of the town, one night last week, after reading several columns in a Boston daily about murders, suicides, executions, burglaries, etc., retired for the night, and shortly passed into 'the arms of Morpheus.' But those horrid crimes were still fresh in his imagination. He fancied the burglars were trying to force an entrance into the room by one of the windows, and in repelling the attack before waking he broke seven lights of glass, taking sash and all, and cutting his hand badly. 'Clark' thinks there would really be less danger in attacking actual burglars."

June 18, 1879: "Some folks think that if they twist a person's toe when they commence talking in their sleep, he or she will tell all they know. 'Charley' tells of a young man who recently tried this experiment while assisting his mother in 'watching' with a sick young woman. It resulted in the experimenter receiving a kick that sent him sprawling on the floor."

December 29, 1880: "We heard of a party who are now sleeping on the floor, having accidentally broken down the bedstead, and being too modest to get it replaced, as the boys might find it out."

September 6, 1882: "A vendor of soap undertook to sell grease eradicating soap on the street, when some hoodlums began to throw apples and stones at him. He was quite sharply assailed when one of the

Left, Lyman Wheelock's home; *right*, Wheelock office building, presently Barre Senior Citizens headquarters. Picture taken circa 1886. *Aldrich Library Collection.*

special policemen, recently appointed, who is himself a seller of soap, ordered the street vendor to leave town which he proceeded to do. This is the story of the boys, the other side claim that the soap vendor sang bawdy songs which caused the boys to throw apples, and then the soap man drew a revolver, whereupon the policeman ordered him to leave town. Those are the two stories."

August 4, 1886: "The style of hair cut at present is pompadour, and the heads of a number of the boys look like the back of an irritated porcupine. The girls are not so in love with this style, for they say the hair sticks into their necks about 11 o'clock, and does not feel half so nice as it did before. 'Harry' is responsible to a large extent for introducing this barbaric style of hair dress, but it is done nicely, and the boys are pleased if the girls are not."

December 22, 1886: "A certain young lady and gentleman were out riding the other evening, and, noticing that the horse made quite hard work of drawing the sleigh, the lady turned to her companion and asked if it would not lighten the load if she were to sit in his lap. Fact."

April 6, 1887: "One of 'the boys' hired a livery team, and drove to Montpelier last Saturday. Capital liquid refreshment, taken by the horse probably, caused a tip-over and runaway, on the return trip, which resulted in a somewhat dilapidated sleigh, and the horse reaching Barre an hour before its driver."

December 4, 1889: "Perrin Bancroft has of late noticed that his cows were dry in the morning, and naturally supposed that some one with a healthy appetite for milk was robbing him of the supply of lacteal fluid which his herd was wont to give. He determined to catch the marauder flagrante delicto. So one night last week he secreted himself in the barn and awaited developments. For a long time all was still. No sound was heard save a whispered conversation between the Hay-tender and the Pitchfork, mingled with loose remarks from the Rake, and sarcastic replies from the Pitchfork. 'Suddenly there came a tapping/As of some one gently lapping/Water from a barrel standing just foreinst the wide barn door.' Mr. Bancroft thought of Poe, and then of his cows. Striking a light he approached the spot where his lowing cows were lying low, and found to his amusement that each cow was standing treat for a pig. A space at one end of the barn had been finished off for a drove of pigs, and they had broken through into the cows' quarters and helped themselves to all the milk on the premises. Mr. Bancroft has shut off the free lunch arrangement as he proposes to have the milk for his own use in the future."

September 10, 1890: "It is not considered safe to ask Henry J. Smith the price of bull dogs just at this time. A new collar and chain is all he has left of a fine one imported from Boston last week, the animal slipping its collar and taking its departure from Barre."

January 24, 1891: "The boys are making life a burden for 'Professor' Lascor these days, because of a trip he took to Northfield last Saturday. To get even for several jokes perpetrated by Lascor, a decoy letter, purporting to be written by a young lady asking him to meet her at Northfield, was sent to Lascor, and he swallowed the bait without even chewing it."

July 12, 1892: "The hot water front of the city restaurant range exploded Saturday morning while the girls were getting breakfast, blowing the door of the firebox open and distributing coals, ashes and water clear to the office. No one was hurt, but the amount of female horror that blew into the office at the same time, mingled with pale faces and erect auburn locks was equal to a three mice scare."

July 12, 1893: "The story of the cow that jumped over the moon is familiar to all, but the latest cow to achieve notoriety is one belonging to Charles Barber, which undertook to jump Barber's hired man over the Barre post-office one day last week. He was leading the animal along, when she suddenly slipped and fell, pushing her head between the man's legs. She got up just as suddenly, to his sorrow and mortification, as well as to the intense and absorbing interest of the bystanders, and when he realized where he was he sat in the middle of the street a couple of blocks away—more or less—with an expression on his face akin to that worn by a western baseball empire."

April 8, 1896: "Alexander Peters is a scientist. One day last week he was found crawling on his stomach on Main street, studying the Darwinian theory that man at one time got around on all fours. One of the officers did not quite appreciate the attention he was attracting in his experiments, and arrested him. In the city court he laid the blame on his wife, and said that she gave him liquor, and when he became filled shut off the supply."

Of course, a good deal of the "Barre Bundle" consisted of news told in a fairly straightforward manner, if with occasionally something of a

All eyes are on the race at Barre Trotting Park, 1888. It is currently the site of Spaulding High School's Pendo Field. *Aldrich Library Collection.*

wink. With a new bandstand installed in the village park in 1878, it was remarked on June 26 that "since the completion of the new band stand, the boys have favored the people with an open air concert every Saturday night, and will continue to do so during the summer. They play well, and are improving fast. The most they need now is a teacher."

Levi J. Bolster, a successful owner of businesses, tenements and various real estate throughout the city, was often mentioned by the Bundler. Bolster was apparently known as a shrewd man with something of a temper. On April 23, 1879, the Bundler declared, "Bolster is expecting a carload of croquet sets from Randolph, to be used by those who he has driven out of business, it is said."

Bolster was featured again on November 4, 1891: "L.J. Bolster and George C. Mackie had an altercation last Monday over the ownership of some land near the works of Jones Brothers. The guys of the derrick owned by Mackie reached over upon land owned by Bolster, and he attempted to remove them, the result being that he was landed by Mackie on a pile of stone, with a dislocated shoulder."

The issue of February 16, 1887, featured this item that did not necessarily reflect well on Bolster:

> *Barre has been wrought up to quite a pitch of excitement because of a row that occurred last Saturday between L.J. Bolster and Miss Fannie Hutchinson, in the millinery store of the latter. For some time past children living in Central Place have been sliding between the Wood block and the tenement owned by Mr. Bolster. W.F. Scott, of the* Enterprise, *and Mrs. Scott objected to the sliding, and did what they could to prevent it, frequently sprinkling ashes on the sliding place, when the children would draw on snow, and continue the sport. According to the story of Miss Hutchinson, Mr. Scott asked Mr. Bolster to see if he could not put a quietus on the sliding. It is claimed that the land between the two buildings is owned by Mr. Bolster, and according to his story the snow that had been drawn upon the sliding place has been raised to such a height that when it thawed water was washed into the lower tenement. Saturday last Mr. Bolster went to Central Place, and tacked up a notice forbidding further sliding. While he was there engaged it is claimed that Mrs. Heber Perley, who lives in the Wood block, and has two children*

who have been engaged in the sliding, talked to her son, upholding him in his course. Thinking that perhaps a verbal order not to slide might be necessary, Mr. Bolster went into the store of Miss Hutchinson, to inform Mrs. Perley of the new order of things, when he was ordered from the store by the proprietor. Not moving quick enough to please her, she is alleged to have struck him in the face, and broken the skin on his nose. Then he took Miss Hutchinson by the wrists, and held on until her anger had somewhat subsided. This is the Bolster version. On the other hand Miss Hutchinson claims that when Mr. Bolster entered her store he used very abusive language, and because of this she ordered him to leave. This he absolutely refused to do, when she took him by the lapel of his coat, and turned him towards the door. She was then struck on one shoulder and grabbed by one wrist, when she struck him with the back of the other hand, but not sufficiently hard to make even a mark. She was then grabbed by both wrists, backed against the counter, and so hard did he press his finger nails into her flesh that black and blue marks were produced. After being released she says she went into her bed-room, followed by Mr. Bolster, who still refused to leave, but when she informed him he was in her private room he went out.

The Bundler himself was a target of Bolster's ire, as noted on January 2, 1884: "L.J. Bolster 'sweetly' remarked of the writer while in the former's store Saturday, 'when they started to make him, they were a little out of stock!' As this was about the only smart thing heard said during four hours sojourn in Barre that day, it is duly put on record." And then there's this odd item from July 9 of the same year: "L.J. Bolster claims that he owns the horse whose tail was recently cut off by parties returning from Montpelier, and says he hired the boys to do it, as he wanted a horse with a tail in the English style."

As much as the Bundler enjoyed relaying gossip and the foibles of many Barre residents, he was also something of a Barre booster, being sure to note when instances of good citizenship occurred or when a local merchant met with success. For example, the following report appeared on September 17, 1879: "Last week a runner from Lowell, Mass., visited town, and sold belting to the Fork Factory company. He came all the way on a bicycle, stopping to sell his goods. He said he could travel seventy-five miles a day in this way, without expense of horse keeping, carrying his samples strapped to the bicycle. He left for Wells River last Saturday afternoon."

An item from March 17, 1880, told of the inventiveness of some local businessmen: "Telephones have been put up to connect the stores of J.M. Perry and W.H. Gladding with their residences, which are working successfully. Others have ordered instruments. George W. Jackman, of Waterbury, did the work. His father suggests that Dr. Gladding had his put up so that he could hear the baby when it cries."

On at least one occasion, a resident's inventiveness landed him in trouble. From June 28, 1882: "As is known to most of the people of the village Perley Chandler, the ingenious jeweler, has had telephone connections between his store and house for some time, using machines of his own manufacture. Recently A.C. Brown, agent of the Bell Telephone Co., for Washington county, got his eye on the wire and traced it to the store of Mr. Chandler, where he found that the patents of the Bell Telephone Co. were being infringed on by machines made wholly by Mr. Chandler. Consequently the latter has been notified to destroy or give up the machines at once, or be prosecuted, which seems rather hard, but there is probably no way to dodge it."

The booming granite industry was the subject of this item from June 13, 1883: "There are now sixteen quarries opened in town, four of which supply the larger part of the granite sent to market. Twenty-five different dealers are engaged in the granite business. The largest establishment employs eighty men constantly, another forty-five, and others from twenty-five down. Total number employed in the industry, about 335, exclusive of teamsters. The annual sales of granite are estimated at not less than $200,000."

The housing market was also subject to comment. On March 17, 1886, the Bundler predicted: "A building boom is to strike Barre in the spring, and houses are to go up in every direction. Should the town continue to grow as it has in the past year, it will embarrass the Selectmen to find time to name the streets." Also of interest, from November 3, 1886: "The Widow Packard has deviated somewhat from the general course pursued by others of her sex, and is managing a business that would puzzle many a man to transact equally as well. She has built two tenements on Main street, which she is renting to good advantage, and the past season has had her own residence thoroughly remodeled in an attractive and convenient way. She contemplates building two more tenements in the spring, and is of the opinion that her money is better invested in this way than to let it lie idle, doing no-one any good."

But, lest one assume that Barre was always bustling and forward thinking, we also present this item from June 2, 1886, which should have an oddly familiar ring to those of us living more than a century later: "The arrival of a barrel of kerosene oil last week seems to have killed all interest in the electric light question. Some people are enthusiastic enough in almost any enterprise until it taxes their pocket, and when it reaches that point their enthusiasm takes sudden flight. There are those who will probably always stick to petroleum, but at the same time the truly enterprising ones are keeping their eyes open to progression, and it can be expected that electric light will illuminate the streets and business places before a century has passed away."

Similar instances abound of the sympathetic Bundler attempting to reform Barre by pointing out the faults of its citizens or of its governance. A sampling follows:

George Mackie's new home, corner of Washington and Mount Streets. *Aldrich Library Collection.*

May 22, 1878: "If those men who race their horses through the streets would provide a street sprinkler, and keep the dust wet down, the town authorities might allow them to keep on racing, for we need the sprinkler very much."

December 2, 1885: "It is said that several of the ladies have been insulted on the streets during past evenings, by those of the masculine gender who had probably been imbibing too much of the ardent. One lady was recently so badly frightened that she slipped and fell on the sidewalk, which caused her to be confined to the house by illness for several days. It appears as if two policemen were not enough for Barre."

June 15, 1887: "A gentleman down from New York, while visiting in town recently, drove past the cemetery. Seeing a clothes line filled with the weeks washing in that enclosure, he remarked that during many years travel both in this country and abroad he had never seen anything like this. It is to be hoped that the Cemetery Commissioners will promptly abate the nuisance."

October 9, 1889: "The mud in the streets of Barre—but why speak of it again. It has been told in song and story many times. Nevertheless it is disgraceful, and it would seem as though there must be some remedy."

June 18, 1890: "Some inoffensive Italians were fishing in the river below the village last Sunday, when a gang of hoodlums began throwing stones in the water to frighten the fish. One Italian was hit on the forehead with a sharp stone, cutting a gash that required surgical aid. No arrests were made."

August 6, 1890: "One of the prisoners brought before Justice W.E. Barney last Monday morning, showed the effects of being confined in the Barre lock-up. His coat was covered with soil and filth, and it is said that a swarm of rats make the place a terror to the unfortunates who are obliged to be incarcerated there. Barre ought to provide a decent place for her criminals."

October 22, 1890: "The crossings of Barre streets are in an execrable position, being covered with several inches of mud, and those who attended divine service last Sunday had ample ground for the complaints they made. With fine concrete walks and pavements, it seems shortsighted economy for the village fathers to allow the crossings to remain in such a wretched condition."

Looking up Washington Street to Spaulding Graded School, 1893. The building is currently home to the Vermont History Center. *Aldrich Library Collection.*

September 11, 1895: "H.A. Rugg continues to cover the town with posters, although the city council has again refused to give him a bill poster's license. Mr. Rugg is courting a test with the city, but it does not at present appear to be forthcoming. Mr. Rugg was seen by the *Argus and Patriot* scribe on Tuesday while at work in front of his bill boards and said he knew the city council had refused a second application for a license, but he would continue to post bills until he was stopped. He appeared anxious to have the city test the case and said he was taking this course by advice of good authority. 'Look at that Barre Breeders' association bill on my boards,' he said, 'what kind of gall do you call that, after they advertised a short time ago that H.A. Rugg had no connection with their society? If I don't make that bill look sick before the day is over my name ain't Rugg. I won't tear it down, either, but there will be a deep mourning around it by to-morrow.' Mr. Rugg is billing the town for Blanchard's Opera house, and says that a special train will be run to Barre after the performance of 'The Girl I Left Behind Me.'"

Chapter 2

"Talk of the Town" and "Sparks of Granite City"

1897–1910

With the arrival of a daily newspaper in Barre, the shape of the local correspondents' column was transformed. While the *Argus & Patriot*'s "Barre Bundle" had included all news from Barre, both important and trivial, the writer of "Talk of the Town" was given more leeway to concentrate on the trivial, as the important news was elsewhere in the paper. During its early years, "Talk of the Town" was subtitled "Local Happenings of the Day Briefly Told." Perhaps because it suited the typesetter, each item was a little lengthier than the one above it. For example, here are some of the items, listed in order, from the issue of April 12, 1897:

"A.F. Sortwell was in the city Sunday.

"A child of John Forbes' is sick with the measles.

"Harry Brown of Waterbury was in the city Saturday.

"Chas. Hattoon of Vershire is visiting Joseph Denno.

"Another Celestial has joined his countrymen in this city.

"Alex Anderson, 2d, has moved from Silver to Camp street.

"Dr. D.J. Smith, veterinary, was in St. Johnsbury recently.

"Wm. Stevens has moved from Beckley street to Merchant street.

"The Knights of Pythias will hold a whist party in their hall this evening.

"The Barre juniors' base-ball team has about $30 subscribed for its benefit.

"H.K. Huntington of West Fairlee is visiting his daughter, Mrs. F.A. Gove.

"Born, to Mr. and Mrs. J.F. McDonnell of Branch street, a son, this morning.

"Miss Mary West has returned from Waterbury, where she has been visiting.

"E.A. Chittendon, traffic manager of the Central Vermont, was in the city last Saturday.

"Guy Humphrey of Waterbury was in the city recently, visiting his brothers, Bert and Charles.

"Miss Alice Haven left for Jaffrey, N.H., today. She has been visiting Mrs. J.M. Eastman.

"Joseph Donnolley has returned from Bolton, where he has been laboring the past winter.

"Oscar Carleton, Jr., of Laconia, N.H., is working with his uncle, Frank Carleton, painting.

"Col. E.A. Crittendon, general agent for the Central Vermont railroad, was in the city Saturday.

"F.W. Ward who has been spending a few days in the city, returned to Burlington this morning.

"S. Hollister Jackson went back to Burlington today to resume his college work. A.O. Smith went back Saturday.

"O.H. Hale has purchased the old Armory building, in the rear of the Wheelock place for an auction room. He will open up this week.

"J. Henry Jackson went last Saturday to Burlington, to begin his course of lectures in the medical department of the University of Vermont.

"Howard Holden, a civil engineer, of Revere, Mass., is in the city today in consultation with the street commissioners. Mr. Holden is a son of Eli Holden of this city.

"Z. Macchi, the stoneman, is to build another stone-shed near his present one on Second street. It will be 36 feet long and 24 wide and will be fitted up with all the modern appliances of the stone business.

"A settlement has been made between Nelson Phelps and the Baltimore & Ohio railroad, for injuries he received in the recent railroad wreck. Mr. Phelps went Saturday to Petersboro, N.H., to visit Mrs. Phelps.

"Quite an unusual sight this forenoon was a long line of six-horse stone teams, heavily loaded, going down Main street, like a funeral procession. But it didn't look like the funeral of the granite business, by any means.

"Sidney Smith, ex–city engineer of Rutland, who was turned down this year because that city thought him too expensive, is in the city today. It is stated on good authority that Mr. Smith will make no bid for the position of city engineer here.

"Mr. and Mrs. Eustice Ritchie were given a surprise party Friday evening at the home of Francis Leith. There were about 25 present and an enjoyable evening was passed. There was music for entertainment and lunch was served. Mr. and Mrs. Ritchie were presented a large Saratoga trunk."

The above twenty-nine items give at least some idea of what "Talk of the Town" would continue to be throughout its long career. Twelve of the items concerned persons visiting Barre; in two such cases, a reason beyond "paying a call" to someone was detailed. One was about a sick person; one was about a birth; one was about a new resident, the "Celestial"; two were about people moving from one part of the city to another; five were about Barre residents going to or coming from other places; two concerned the doings of local organizations; three concerned local businesses or business conditions; two were at least tangentially concerned with legal or political issues; and one was about a social event.

Considerably more than half of the items concerned what might be termed "comings and goings." An assumption can be made that a daily canvass of the entire city's population was not made for the purpose of "Talk of the Town," but it might be considered rash to speculate about the criteria for inclusion. However, it appears as if many of the people mentioned have their profession or ranking in society named, and we can count some doctors, a college student, at least two businessmen and a couple of engineers. True to his identification here, O.H. Hale was an auctioneer for most of his life in Barre. S. Hollister Jackson became a lawyer and eventually attained the office of Vermont's lieutenant governor. Interestingly, while there seems to be a general effort to name all appropriate people tied to events, an exception was made for the "Celestial." Perhaps we can be grateful that, unlike the Barre Bundler, this author did not refer to the unnamed person as "almond-eyed."

The *Barre Evening Telegram*'s column, "Sparks from the Granite City," is so similar in style and content to "Talk of the Town" as to render superfluous a sample of one day's work. It should merely be noted that all items from 1898 to 1902 are from the *Telegram*, and the remainder are from the *Daily Times*. This author's remarks, clarifications and more are in brackets.

July 6, 1897: "The old house in Berlin that was occupied by Mrs. Harroun until her death was burned down last Saturday evening. Some over-enthusiastic boys thought it would make a good bonfire and no one interfered to put the fire out when once started."

September 10, 1897: "All foot-ball cranks who care to know the rules of the game can obtain a full set at Frank McWhorter's store free of charge."

November 11, 1897: "City Engineer C.S. Currier will make his first and only appearance this season as the coy and innocent maiden, Dorothy, in the farce at the minstrel show, Nov. 23d. Dorothy gets a first mortgage on the heart of the clerk in Phelps Bros. store and undertakes to foreclose. Her innocent ways can be seen only at the minstrel show."

Currier Park, circa 1899. Mary Baker Eddy briefly lived here but was driven out by the sound of the village band's frequent practice sessions. *Vermont Historical Society.*

April 22, 1898: "The members of the Barre Civic Federation of Woman's Clubs have taken a great interest in the affairs of the city. They have a movement on foot whereby they are going to try and beautify the city by having the City Park put in a good shape. They propose to have concrete walks laid through the park and have the trees trimmed and those that are decayed will be cut down. They also propose to have the railing on the northerly side of the park taken down. If the ladies' ideas are carried out, flower-beds will be laid out and the park will be put in first-class shape, which will be a credit to the city. It is earnestly hoped that the ladies will succeed in carrying out their plans."

June 27, 1898: [Fairly often, the column writers would make what might be termed broad hints as to the preferred action of certain citizens.] "D.M. Miles is thinking very strongly of making his new block five stores high. He has not fully decided yet but the chances are that it will be done. There will be an elevator in the building and the fifth floor would doubtless rent to good advantage."

[On June 29, 1898, regular trolley car (or "electrics") service began between Barre and Vermont's capital city, Montpelier, seven miles away.]

July 19, 1898: "A live wire came in contact with one of the trolley wire poles on Washington street last night and created a considerable blaze."

September 15, 1898: "The residents at the farther end of Merchant street are kicking vigorously because the concrete sidewalk has not been finished. About half has been done and the remainder is unfinished." [Oddly, the upper portion of Merchant Street still has no sidewalk in 2011!]

November 4, 1898: "The farmers who drive here to do their trading are highly indignant because there are no places to hitch horses along the streets. At present they are obliged to bring their wives along for hitching posts. The ladies are getting sick of this kind of business, and who can blame them. It does seem as though there might be a place somewhere to hitch horses."

February 4, 1899: [Barre's city hall and opera house had burned on January 18, 1898. The building to replace it was not completed until August 1899, and the *Telegram* was pessimistic about how it would turn out.] "Often in years gone by the citizens of Barre have seen our officials spend large sums of money in certain directions only to all regret it in a few weeks. We are spending a large sum of money for a new city hall building and opera house combined, only to some day be alive to regret the blunder which competent men say is being made in connection with the stage."

July 29, 1899: "Geo. T. Conner who has the contract for furnishing the boxes and the stage and hall carpets expects that the brass work and the carpets will arrive here Monday. The drapery for the boxes is already here and it is very beautiful in design and the boxes of the opera house will be especially attractive."

August 25, 1899: "One thing that is needed at the new city hall is some guards over one of the windows of the city engineer's office, so that when trunks etc. are hoisted into the opera house the windows will not get smashed. One has already had a trunk bump against it."

September 15, 1899: "A firm from Boston has opened for a short time a gallery in Miles' old block, 124 No. Main St. and are taking beautiful photographs at one cent each. Many people have already taken advantage of this great opportunity. Get your photographs taken without delay. Pictures taken just as good on cloudy days by this new process. Bring your babies and children. Miles' old block, Pennygraph Company."

October 16, 1899: "Haymarket square, or the 'Forum,' as the territory next to Massucco's fruit store is sometimes called, was the scene of gayety Saturday night. Fruit venders, cane ringers, hammer throwers, etc., attracted a large crowd."

February 27, 1900: "The Italians of Barre gave the drama entitled 'Antonio Gasparani' in the opera house last night to a large audience. The play was in six acts. It was something new in this city being given in the Italian language. There was a large cast of well-known Italian people. The Transatlantic band furnished music."

March 9, 1900: "The damages from the recent explosion in William Miers' barber shop have been repaired on the inside. Mr. Miers has had a new water heating apparatus put in, and his rooms are once more in a condition for public patronage."

April 12, 1900: "Some enterprising person has tapped all the maple trees in Elmwood cemetery and is doing a thriving business in the manufacture of maple sugar."

May 8, 1900: "The many friends in this city of William Kendrick who went to California a few months ago will be pleased to learn that he has

Newsboys and others pose near Depot Square, summer 1906. *Vermont Historical Society.*

secured a lucrative position in a drug store at Whittier, Cal., and that he is residing with W.L. Stafford, a former resident of this city who is now a hotel proprietor at Whittier."

August 17, 1900: "H.E. Cutler has just finished up some fine photographs from negatives that he recently took of Barre City from Hooker Hill, that are the finest birdseye pictures we have ever seen. The day was exceptionally clear when the negatives were taken, and the city and distant hills are all sharp and clear. He will be pleased to show them to anyone interested in Barre City of today."

September 10, 1900: "A child fell one story out of the Tomasi block yesterday afternoon, but he got up and ran away so he was probably uninjured."

November 30, 1900: "G.J. Hawes had a family Thanksgiving dinner in his restaurant yesterday, with all the Hawes family, young and old, present."

December 15, 1900: "The services in the Salvation Army tomorrow will be conducted by Capt. E.W. Owen. The subject for the evening service, 'The Unpardonable Sin.' There will also be a special time tonight with selections by the gramophone, etc. The services are held in the old city hall which is now properly seated."

March 12, 1901: "Photographer Cutler was down before the county court today with the pictures he recently took of the vicinity where Patrick Brown was when he was shot." [Patrick Brown, Barre's chief of police, was shot, allegedly by two anarchists, on the night of December 27, 1900. Brown reportedly went on to Buffalo after President McKinley had been shot to share his wisdom on the shooting habits of anarchists.]

May 1, 1901: "Alexander H. Findlay, the well known golf expert with Wright & Ditson, Boston, will arrive here tomorrow afternoon to lay out the golf links at Cherryvale. The golf club will hold a meeting at the Universalist parsonage at 8 o'clock tomorrow evening to adopt a constitution and elect officers. Mr. Findlay will be present."

June 6, 1901: "The city is doing a fine job on the Summer street ledge and the material taken away to widen the street there is being used to bring Pearl street up to grade. It is to be hoped that if the work of widening Summer street is not all completed when the appropriation is used up, that another small appropriation will be made."

July 13, 1901: "Acting on orders from City Attorney Wishart, Chief of Police Brown notified the old organ grinder and his wife to leave the city at once. This notice was given them Thursday evening and they departed yesterday morning on a car for Montpelier. The couple were one of the greatest nuisances that the city has had in a long while. They were dressed in rags and both pretended to be cripples. During the daytime they would grind their hand organ all right, taking care to keep on the back streets, but at night they would take a position on Main street and turn their organ so that it made only the most doleful discords. Mr. Wishart heard that they had been driven out of Burlington because they had money, and so were not in need of charity. He investigated and found the story true. Accordingly he notified them to get out of the city under penalty of being arrested if they did not obey. They are the same people who have been in this city several times in the past year or so."

March 8, 1902: "The owner of the Gertrude Coghlan Co., which appeared here last week, has written Manager Lapoint, asking for information concerning the transactions of the company while in this city, as Will P. Webster, who was acting manager of the company, has been missing since last week Friday, as are also the funds of the company. The company is still on tour, having ample capital."

May 26, 1902: "When Otto Lewis was leaning out of the window in the opera house that is used for the baggage he fell to the ground a distance of some 60 feet, about 7:30 o'clock Saturday evening. He struck upon his feet and fell over on his back. Water Superintendent W.J. Campbell took him to his home on Ayers St., in his carriage and Dr. M.L. Chandler, who was summoned, found no bones broken. Yesterday Lewis was reported as better although he was badly bruised and shaken up by the experience."

July 18, 1902: "Frank W. Nichols has sold his motor cycle to Frank Burgess. He had already ordered another. Mr. Burgess is much pleased with his purchase and rode to North Randolph on it last Sunday. If it is pleasant Sunday he will ride to White River Junction on it."

December 6, 1902: "A disagreeable feature of the entertainment at the opera house last night was the competition that one or two women from out of town set up against the stage artists. During the pathetic part of the play these visitors in order that the other members of the audience might not be impressed to the point of shedding tears broke into loud bursts of laughter and during the time that they were not hilarious they were engaged in discussing various topics of personal interest in voices loud enough to prevent all others in their vicinity from hearing much of anything that was said on the stage. The tumult subsided to some extent after head usher Averill gave them some instructions as to the proprieties of the occasion."

[In 1903, on Town Meeting Day—traditionally the first Tuesday of March—Vermont voters were allowed to vote on whether to allow their communities to open saloons. This was known as "local option" or license. Barre voters approved "license" in 1903 and 1904 and from 1916 to 1919. Barre only voted yes for license once between 1905 and 1915, in 1907. Assuredly, most Barre drinkers had no problem getting their liquor during nonlicense years, either through drugstores' "medicinal" alcohol or from the many informal speakeasies, usually located in kitchens of private homes.]

May 27, 1903: "A man who was suspected of being one of the firebugs who set fire to the Tilden house a few days ago was arrested at Bethel yesterday, but was allowed to go as there was no evidence on which to hold him for the offense."

June 15, 1903: "The merchants on the west side of Main street are requested to keep their teams alongside, and not backed to the curbing while the surface sewer on that street is under construction. The street is blocked to a large extent by the throwing up of dirt."

September 2, 1903: "The gang of about twenty five workmen who are at work on Main street enjoyed a few minutes rest yesterday afternoon and had their pictures taken in the street at the corner of Washington and Main streets by Photographer F.C. Eaton. Included in the picture were the street commissioners of the city, Street Superintendent Alex Bruce, City Engineer Allen, Mayor Jackson and ex-Mayor Melcher." [The work consisted of paving a portion of North Main Street with granite blocks.]

October 15, 1903: "Those Barre people who are not so fortunate as to be the possessors of automobiles smiled yesterday afternoon when they saw one of the 'horseless carriages' dragged down Main street behind a heavy stone team. This was one of those times when the auto gives out and leaves the driver stranded where it stops. The driver of the machine seemed to have an occupied expression."

February 23, 1904: "A large number of block owners along Main street are making repairs to comply with the law requiring doors to swing outward. Those who have complied are H.O. Worthen, J.W. Gordon, L.M. Averill, Eastman Bros., J.B. Sanguinetti and the Tomasi block."

March 29, 1904: "Montpelier will have an automobile hack when the $1,350 Rambler touring car which Jake Galuiski has purchased arrives. The car will carry five passengers. It will be a novelty in the hack line."

April 11, 1904: "The Main street sewer pipe, near Second street has sprung a leak, and the street department has begun digging up the street to make repairs. In order to prevent interruption of street car traffic a car will be kept on this end of the line, to and from which passengers may transfer."

June 16, 1904: "Clarence A. Dodge of Berlin, the well known golf player, and Miss Myrtle Woodworth of Barton, were married at that place yesterday, the Rev. Mr. Johnson performing the ceremony. Mr. and Mrs. Dodge came to Berlin today and will make their future home in the new house being erected near his father's on the Montpelier road."

July 9, 1904: "About 150 people eagerly watched the bulletin board in front of the Hotel Northern yesterday afternoon while the games were in progress. At times excitement ran high and one listening to the cheers might agree that an actual game was in progress."

August 15, 1904: "J.W. Gordon today received a large Haynes-Apperson automobile which he recently purchased. It is a gasoline car and the first of its kind to be owned in Barre. This makes a total of about 25 cars in this city."

October 12, 1904: "Along about dusk yesterday the electric railroad's 'abandoned' car was attached by tow to the repair car and drawn to the car barn, and a section of Main street which has been occupied by the company for two weeks or more was finally given up to its rightful owner, the public."

January 20, 1905: "We wish to inform the people of Barre that we have moved our stock of goods from the A. Tomasi block to the Co-operative store, 303 N. Main street. We have been refused permission to move our sign, but we are not located in the A. Tomasi block. Meaker Bros." [By this time, many "Talk of the Town" items were short advertisements.]

February 17, 1905: "A man drove up to the city watering trough near the park this forenoon with barrels, washtubs and jars, and proceeded to fill the receptacles with water. He was one of those whose water supply has been cut short by the frost. The city water teams are going the rounds of the city supplying those who are in a similar position."

March 28, 1905: "The painting of the figure of a stonecutter by the artist, Souverine, is completed and is now on exhibition in the show window of B.W. Hooker & Co., where it is attracting a good deal of attention. The expression of the face is particularly commented upon as being a clever piece of work. The painting represents a man, stripped to the waist, hammer and chisel in hand and standing beside a large stone."

April 14, 1905: "The old house on the library lot at the corner of Elm and Washington streets has been secured by a new religious society in town, the Mission and General Assembly of the Church of the First Born, and the first services will be held there Sunday forenoon, afternoon and evening. The building will be repaired for the society."

July 21, 1905: "Open air concert rear of Pavilion both Friday and Saturday night. Agreeable parties, lots of fun and bargains. O.H. Hale, Auctioneer."

Residents and others lounge on what appears to be a hot day in City Park, circa 1909. The fountain's place is currently occupied by a bandstand. *Aldrich Library Collection.*

September 11, 1905: "The advance agent for 'Ikey and Abey,' which showed at the opera house Saturday evening, announced that the show was being tried out on the road before going into Boston. Our advice to it is, keep out of Boston. While the company contained some clever people, the show is poor and in spots vulgar. There was very little fun to it, though the singing was generally good."

October 17, 1905: "'I guess we've got about 130 people on this car,' said the motorman of a Barre and Montpelier trolley as he surveyed the jammed and jamming crowd on his conveyance the other day. Men, women and children were hanging on, for all the world like brown-tail moths clinging to a tree. Where there was room for a foot and a grip for a hand there was a passenger. The normal capacity of one of the cars is 50 people. The conductor went through the car and rang up 135 fares, while two 'deadheads' were also occupying space, making a total of 137. The carmen have got so accustomed to carrying big crowds that they are pretty accurate on an estimate. 'That's nothing,' declared the motorman, when the conductor had finished ringing up the 135 fares. 'I've carried 172 and 173 people on successive trips.' The road has given up the practice of allowing people to ride on the fenders, however."

January 31, 1906: "John W. Gordon's automobile enthusiasm got the better of him yesterday afternoon and he brought out his Haynes-Apperson from the garage and took a spin about the city and the surrounding territory. The trip was enjoyable except for the fact that he encountered considerable mud, especially outside the city."

March 10, 1906: "Annie Rhind, the daughter of James Rhind of Brook street, is not accustomed to seeing negroes. She is only ten years old and there are not many colored people in Barre. She was walking home late yesterday afternoon and was just passing the Tomasi block at the corner of North Main and Seminary streets when a big negro loomed into view. The sight so terrified the little girl that she tumbled off the sidewalk and down into the basement entrance of the Tomasi building, striking on her shoulders and face. Annie was picked up and carried to her home. It is thought that a big, deep cut on one side of her face is the extent of her injuries, which is very fortunate as the fall which she took was about ten feet to a stone basement."

April 13, 1906: "A local golf enthusiast went down to the Barre Golf Club links yesterday afternoon and found the grounds in anything but playable shape. A heavy coating of ice made the game impossible yesterday and will, in fact, postpone the opening of the sport to a time much later than usual. When the season gets started the local club hopes to arrange frequent matches with other clubs in this section."

May 7, 1906: "The 'coo-ing seats' have been placed in the City Park and the drinking fountain has been uncorked, so that summer may be considered as really begun."

September 15, 1906: "George E. Hooker of Chicago arrived in the city today for a few days' visit with his brother, B.W. Hooker, and sister, Mrs. Minnie M. Wheeler. Mr. Hooker is on his return trip to Chicago from a two months' trip abroad where he has been studying the conditions of municipal ownership of electric railways and tramways for the City Club of Chicago, of which he is secretary." [Hooker lived at Jane Addams's famous Hull House in Chicago from 1899 to 1939.]

November 20, 1906: "While looking around for liquor yesterday afternoon in the third story of the Bolster building on Main street deputies

Slayton, Camp and Lawson ran into a game of cards, five hundred chips and a machine which was a new one on the officers. They couldn't name the machine and didn't molest it. The chips were made for the machine. The men found in the place were not playing the machine but were matched up in a game of cards which goes as legitimate, so they were not hindered. However, their names are in the possession of the officers. No liquor was found. The warrant was issued by Grand Juror E.R. Davis."

January 15, 1907: "A. Tomasi's bronco caused considerable amusement to people who happened around Depot square this morning while the owner was attempting to do the bronco buster's trick of breaking the animal to drive in a sleigh. The bronco wouldn't drive and instead treated the onlookers with a series of side kicks, back kicks, forward kicks and all kinds of manipulations with his legs, finally kicking himself out of the shafts. By this time the owner and five or six men caught hold of the infuriated beast and succeeded in freeing him from the sleigh. To show that he was still master the owner then jumped onto the animal's back and raced him up and down the street."

February 27, 1907: "Emma Goldman, author of 'Mother Earth,' will speak at the Barre opera house tonight, giving her address in English and Luigi Galleani will speak in the Italian language. The posters announcing the meeting state that the purpose is to 'discuss the coming March elections and pirates.'"

April 3, 1907: "Street superintendent Bruce today distributed the rubbish cans, a dozen in number, along Main street, and people are warned to deposit papers and other litter in these receptacles. If they persist in scattering the rubbish on the street as heretofore, there will be prosecutions to follow, so report the city authorities."

September 10, 1907: "Miles' brick block has been put in fine shape, and is ready to let for dancing parties, meetings and other entertainments. An excellent and safe fire escape has been erected at the rear of the building, with entrance into the Gordon block. Orders for the hall will be left at the coal office of D.M. Miles, 122 North Main street, in Moore & Owens' store."

December 6, 1907: "Mack Sennett, who played the part of the sultan in the 'Isle of Bong-Bong,' at the opera house last evening, is a nephew of Mrs. O.N. Granger and visited her during his stay in this city. Mr. Sennett is the son of Mrs. Granger's older sister." [This is the same Mack Sennett who would shortly become a famed movie mogul with Keystone Studios in California. Sennett's niece, Mercedes, was married to prominent Barre citizen Max Holden for several years.]

February 1, 1908: "In spite of the warning of the management of the Fenberg stock company that Friday night's performance, 'The Lamb and the Brute,' would be a gruesome spectacle and that nervous people better keep away, there was naturally a big turnout of people, who wanted their nerves tested. They were tested. The piece is one grand succession of thrills, with a murder every quarter of an hour, and the victims hurled over precipices and stowed away in any little cranny that came convenient. There were several cold chills in the audience, but not a woman needed the ambulance."

April 4, 1908: "There was free eating for everybody on Main street to-day. Dust was the article served up by a boisterous wind, and the clouds

Monument for Barre real estate mogul Levi J. Bolster, Elmwood Cemetery, 1910. *Author's collection.*

of it were so dense at times that people had to take refuge in stores. Ordinarily, dust is not considered an incentive to trade."

October 7, 1908: "A certain automobile in the city should hereafter be an object of terror to the canine pets in the city, as no less than two dogs met their deaths yesterday afternoon under the wheels of the car. The first mortality occurred on Maple Grove street when a young dog owned by Leon Cole ran out at the machine and was run over, crushing out its life. The second dog met its fate on North Main street. The animal ran at the machine and spectators state that the driver tried his best to stop the car before it struck the dog but was unable to do so. The dog was not killed outright but was so badly crushed that Officer Carle put out its life with a shot from his revolver."

November 20, 1908: "Vehicles of all kinds were seen on the streets last evening and to-day. Taking advantage of the snow, many people are driving around in sleighs, which ran smoothly, and the auto enthusiasts are still running their cars around the streets."

December 30, 1908: "Sheet music exchange to be opened Jan. 2, 1909, at 'Tony's' Vermont Fruit Store. Here is the plan: Anyone having sheet music that is not torn or soiled, regardless of what it originally cost them, may exchange it here for something new for the small sum of five cents. There are over 1,500 copies to select from, including some of the latest and best instrumental music and songs, ranging in price from five to seventy-five cents. A special stand in our store will be reserved for this new exchange. This offer may cease without notice. If you have any music that you are tired of or that you don't like, bring it in and take advantage of this opportunity to get something else for it."

January 21, 1909: "The plate glass windows in the front of the Arcade block had a narrow escape from being shattered into pieces at one o'clock this afternoon. A four-horse team of lively horses were being driven up Main street when they met G.A. Wilkinson's automobile. The leaders became frightened at the machine and bolted across the street and headed directly towards the middle window in the front of the block, and they stopped only when their noses hit the glass. Pedestrians helped the driver to get the horses back into the street without any damage being done."

February 10, 1909: "To settle the estate of the late Ephraim French, the lot and house at the corner of North Main and Keith avenue has been placed in the D.A. Perry Real Estate agency for sale. The house is one of the old landmarks in Barre, and the lot, which is 111 feet on Main street by 204 feet on Keith avenue, is one of the most desirable locations for a business block in the city."

April 21, 1909: "Complaints have been made to the police of the marking of store windows on North Main street. At Joseph Merlo's store the name 'Frank' has been scratched on the front window either with a diamond ring or stone of some kind and large circles were cut in the plate glass window in Rouel's barber shop. The police are on the lookout for the offender and if caught the charge against him will be a serious one."

June 21, 1909: "A new make of automobiles for this section was introduced to Barre Saturday when G.H. Bennett received three Interstate machines, made in Muncie, Ind. The cars are 35-horse power and seem to run very smoothly."

July 15, 1909: "Workmen of the street department are slowly pegging away digging up stone chips on North Main street in order that new stone chips in crushed form, may be put in their place. Question: what does the city gain by taking out the old chips and putting in new ones?"

October 14, 1909: "Someone threw a large horse brush through the window of John Berinato's shoe store in the basement of the A. Tomasi block last evening, breaking a large hole in the glass. It was first thought that the window had been broken for the purpose of stealing the shoes from the show window but it was found that none had been taken. The brush was found in front of the window, where it had dropped after striking the glass."

November 24, 1909: "Mrs. Nellie Lawrence Braley of Burlington has shown an interest in the work of beautifying Elmwood cemetery by sending 100 tulips, which have been set out by Supt. Alex. Hanton in a new bed just in front of the tomb, and which will add much to the attractiveness of the cemetery next spring. Then after the tulips have gone by, cannas will be set in the bed for the summer. Several other women have signified their intention of contributing to the beautifying of the cemetery."

January 3, 1910: "Roach Brothers have workmen engaged in removing the front which they placed on the Campbell block when it was opened as a moving picture house. They discontinued it as a picture

Moving the riverbed of the Stevens Branch of the Winooski, near Prospect Street, late 1910. *Aldrich Library Collection.*

show several months ago. The front will be replaced as it was before they hired the place."

February 16, 1910: "The hearing in the case of the state against Mary Estabrooks, charged with keeping a house of ill fame, which was to have been held in city court to-day, was nol prossed this afternoon. The reason for this action was that not sufficient evidence was obtained to warrant hearing the woman on the charge."

March 8, 1910: "Novelli & Calcagni of this city have secured a contract from Mrs. L.J. Bolster of Barre to complete and erect a very fine 'light Barre granite' monument, to be placed at the grave of her late husband in Elmwood cemetery. The quality of the material is to be the finest 'light Barre' that can be obtained, and the work is to be fine 12-cut throughout. The monument is to be of sarcophagus design and elaborately carved. The bottom base will be ten by six and a half by one and a half feet, and the total height of the memorial will be about seventeen feet, including a granite statue representing Meditation. This statue will rest on a plinth at the top of the monument. The work will be one of the finest private monuments in this vicinity, which will mark the progress made in fashioning Barre granite."

June 11, 1910: "One boy, Blossom J. Ossola, broke all records in the public schools of this city during the past school year. He started in last September in the 4th grade, and next fall he starts in the 7th grade. This makes three grades that he has passed in one year, which is an unusually good record and one that is not excelled, if equaled, in the city. Blossom is the son of Joseph D. Ossola of North Main street and was only ten years old last January."

August 25, 1910: "The street railway company hung up small signs to-day, designating the posts where the cars will stop to take on passengers. The signs are small boards, painted white with black letters, 'Cars Stop Here.' The signs are hung on the guide wires which hold the trolley wires from the posts beside the street."

September 8, 1910: "The work was started to-day preparatory to moving the National bank into its new quarters in the Howland block on Saturday."

October 1, 1910: "During the heavy storm this forenoon, hail-stones, almost as large as marbles, pattered on the pavement and in quantities enough to make snow-balling possible."

November 3, 1910: "The American Hotel Specialty Co. of Burlington has placed in the City hotel and the hotel Otis, large automobile maps which will be of value to automobile parties stopping in this city. The map is intended to be a guide to all the good roads in the New England states, the highways which are considered good being marked by heavy lines. The map is encased in an attractive mission frame, and is large enough so that every town and village in the New England states can be seen, and the best roads leading thereto can be easily traced."

Chapter 3

Local News Ascendant

1911–27

By the 1910s, the *Barre Daily Times* was including the local news of many surrounding communities. At least once every two weeks, the following places were posting news: Woodbury, Waitsfield, Randolph, Montpelier, East Barre, East Calais, Worcester, Plainfield, Groton, Hardwick, Williamstown, Northfield, Bethel, Brookfield, South Randolph, Warren, South Woodbury, Middlesex, West Berlin, Chelsea, Marshfield, Orange, South Cabot, Washington, Vershire, Graniteville, South Ryegate, North Montpelier and West Brookfield.

We should add that a good deal of local news was featured in separate news articles. Obituaries, aside from those of the very young or the indigent, were given their own news articles, and any piece of news that was deemed to deserve more than one paragraph also got its own article. A third of the seven-column front page featured local articles, but state, national and international issues were covered as well. Then, as now, national and international news was brought to the reader via the wire services.

How did "Talk of the Town" evolve from its earlier years? In summarizing one column, from June 15, 1911, we should note that fairly early in the history of the column, "Talk of the Town" began featuring short advertisements. While many articles and items boosted local businesses, a certain portion of "Talk of the Town" was composed of actual ads. Six of the examined thirty-two items fall into this category.

Twenty of them concerned "comings and goings" of Barre residents and visitors. The remaining six consisted of five pieces of news about clubs or organizations, and one concerned a funeral.

During the 1911–27 period, Barre City's population stabilized somewhat, and its downtown, which had acquired several major business blocks in the previous years, did not grow substantially. However, by the end of this time, public transit had become much less popular, with automobiles being within the financial reach of all but a small portion of the population. While, as has been demonstrated, "Talk of the Town" was largely devoted to "comings and goings" of no real interest as narrative, it nonetheless managed to include a good deal of anecdotes of at least trivial interest. A selection follows:

January 3, 1911: "The blast in the ledge at the mouth of the new channel was set off yesterday afternoon, and the barrier was practically all blown to pieces, but the rocks choked up the channel so, that a greater part of the stream was held back from entering the channel. Today the men were at work cleaning out the stones with the aid of a derrick." [Some explanation may be in order here: in 1910, it was decided to

For some reason, an automobile is the focus of attention in this photo looking north from City Park, circa 1911. *Author's collection.*

move the channel of the Stevens Branch of the Winooski River for that relatively short span where it was causing problems to the basements of North Main Street business blocks. That is what the "new river channel" refers to above.]

February 20, 1911: "Work at the river-bed excavation is now rapidly nearing completion. The foundation wall and abutments for the bridge are being finished this week, and within a few days it is hoped that the bridge will be moved. Street Commissioner Jesse DeBrune had a gang of men busy this morning unloading a car of spruce planking recently received from Bartlett, N.H. The planks will be laid on the bridge as soon as possible, and Mr. DeBrune expects to complete this part of the change in a day and a night, thereby obstructing traffic for a short time only. The engine, which has been used by the Joseph Long Co., was moved yesterday to the siding and will be shipped soon to Leominster, Mass."

May 15, 1911: "'Baldy,' the valuable bear dog owned by George Bond, met a tragic death on Saturday, when an automobile ran him down in front of the Morse block. He was not killed instantly but died a few minutes later."

June 1, 1911: "It is hardly possible that money is so plenty in Barre that it is being used to fill up the old river bed, but a one-dollar bill was fished out of the water back of Drown's drug store this afternoon. The bill was in plain sight from the rear piazza and looked decidedly tempting regardless of the doubtful debris in which it rested."

July 7, 1911: "Twenty of the laborers, who have been employed by Long & company in the work of changing the river bed, broke up housekeeping in their shacks in the rear of the Allen Lumber company's office last night and left for Boston on the night train. Long & company have practically finished all of the work which they have under personal charge although there is considerable yet to be done by subcontractors. The only work which Mr. Long is superintending now is the erection of the dry wall in the Prospect street cut which is now nearly completed."

October 23, 1911: "Because of a vigorous protest made by some local clergymen and others, work on paving Main street was not conducted yesterday for the first Sunday in several weeks. The clergymen entered protest some days ago, and on Saturday visited various city officials, as a result of which the corner of Main, Elm and Washington streets, where the contractors are now engaged, was a quiet place although the district was so torn up as to be well-nigh impassable. One of the reasons advanced for Sunday work on the streets was that the public necessity required as prompt finishing of the work as possible to avoid the possibility of accidents. The work on the job is now well along. This morning the horse and dog fountain was torn up, so that paving blocks could be laid. A new granite fountain is to be placed on the square, a little nearer the park than the former location."

January 25, 1912: "At a meeting of the library trustees last evening, it was voted to cut down the pine trees in front of the Aldrich library building. The trees are landmarks, having adorned the front yard of David French's property more than half a century ago, but they have declined in the last few years so that one is already dead and the other two are dying out."

February 19, 1912: "Luigi Ares, a mason employed on the new Drown garage, was struck by a beam as it tipped over this afternoon and his right leg was fractured below the knee. Ares was carried to the City hospital in Hooker's ambulance, and the fracture was reduced at once, so that there will be no permanent injury."

April 13, 1912: "Three of the brick cells at the police station were equipped to-day with iron cots to replace the old ones, which had outgrown their usefulness. The new cots are of the same type used in other cells at the station and are designed especially for such purposes. When not in use, the cots can be folded and flattened against the wall of the cells. Three wayfarers who applied to Chief Sinclair for lodging last night, came too early to repose on the new resting places, for they were only installed this morning."

May 23, 1912: "Surveyors have completed plotting the land opposite Jones Bros.' plant preparatory to a big land sale to be held Decoration day and on the following Saturday at 2 o'clock. There are 100 lots in the tract and it is the purpose of the owners to close them all out at auction. Special attractions are to be arranged for the day."

October 3, 1912: "One more club was added to the list of young men's organizations in the city last evening, when the Italian Athletic juniors formed an association which will have club rooms in the Gordon block. The new club starts off with a flourishing membership of some twenty-five members, and it is likely that this number will be materially augmented before the winter months are here. John Sassi is president and O. Cardini is secretary of the club."

December 2, 1912: "The cold weather of Friday and Saturday coated Stevens branch with ice and yesterday a number of skaters went up South Main street to test their equilibrium back of the fork shop. The ice had reached a thickness of nearly two inches and was smooth enough for the most fastidious skater. At Taft's pond on east hill, a small army of skaters gathered Saturday and Sunday. The quiet little lake affords the best skating in the vicinity, it is said, and several hockey matches are slated for the pond this winter."

January 29, 1913: "The erection of the automobile dock at the Montpelier & Wells River freight depot is nearing completion. The new freight pier has been under construction for nearly a week and when

Mrs. H.S. Miles's millinery store, 70 North Main Street, circa 1911. Note the Victrola. *Aldrich Library Collection.*

finished will greatly facilitate the unloading of automobiles consigned to this city. Located at the south end of the freight depot, the pier, about twenty-five feet in length, connects with the main platforms of the depot and runs along side of the spur track, where much of the traffic is deposited. An evenly graded runway slopes from the pier in order that the cars may be unloaded without much labor."

May 12, 1913: "The season's first caravansary of gypsies celebrated their arrival in the city to-day by trying to bolster up the fortune telling business among the more gullible of the villagers. Women dressed in the sombre and dignified colors of the flamingo bird did the business streets during the forenoon selling baskets and other receptacles fashioned by the raffia worker. The peddling of the baskets was obviously a well disguised plan to work the fortune telling gag on the unsuspecting. The band is said to be encamped on the Montpelier road."

July 2, 1913: "A hot weather fever got hold of Louis Romanis' pet sheep yesterday afternoon and before the woolly one from Prospect street could be corralled, he had completed a successful dive through one of the basement windows in the rear of city hall. Mr. Romanis conducts a store on Prospect street and during the long summer afternoons he is wont to tether his abridged flock to a pole in the court at the rear of the store. Yesterday the ram grew peevish over the weather and began to long for an excursion into the unknown world outside the court. Before anyone in the neighborhood could turn a hand to his capture, the ram had shaken tether and was making for the highway. He caromed around the M.&W. freight yards for several moments while an anxious crowd of householders took up the chase. The sheep led his pursuers along Enterprise alley, as the street in the rear of the city building is known, as far as the Blanchard block, where he flanked the crowd at his heels and dove straight through a window into the coal bin in the boiler room. Attaches at city hall extricated the ram from the fuel pile and led him back to his quarters. Mr. Romanis told the chief of police he would call around and pay for the broken glass."

August 6, 1913: "Several stores along North Main street hung out new business cards to-day to replace street signs that had lost their attractiveness through the action of time and the elements. George M. Marrion's Depot square tobacco store is bordered on two sides by a striking sign that has a total length of 63 feet. The gold lettering is done in Roman block style. At the Henry Knight store, a sign measuring 29 feet is lettered in the Roman style. The N.D. Phelps Co. hung out a sign which extends 22 feet across the front. Clipped block letters in gold are used. All three signs, excellent specimens of the sign painters' art, came from the shop of Will Averill."

September 6, 1913: "R. McGaughey and Michael Moore of New York, who are taking cinematograph views in and around Barre for the Kale Co. of Philadelphia, went this morning to the quarries to pass the day. The operators expect to be in Barre several days next week and before they leave the completed films will be shown in a local picture house, it is announced."

November 11, 1913: "Workmen in the employ of the city street department commenced work yesterday to construct a sidewalk along that portion of Summer street known as 'Rocky Ledge,' extending a distance of about 100 feet. During inclement weather pedestrians have been greatly inconvenienced while travelling on the east side of Summer street by reason of the lack of walk along this section. The walk is being made of gravel with cobblestone curbing."

Looking up toward Highland Avenue from Currier Park after a heavy, wet snow, circa 1911. *Aldrich Library Collection.*

January 19, 1914: "A small regiment of skaters thronged the new municipal rink at the Ayers street driving park Sunday afternoon and again in the evening. The ice was even better to-day, for yesterday the water from a stand-pipe at the corner of South Main and Ayers street was still flowing and one end of the enclosure had not frozen sufficiently for skating. Saturday afternoon water connections were made with the North Barre rink on West Second street meadows near the Allen Lumber Co.'s mill. Laborers from the water department shut off the connection this forenoon and if the weather continues cold, the rink will be ready for skating to-morrow morning. Patrons will be asked to assist in the maintenance of each rink whenever snow interferes with the skating."

February 25, 1914: "A new map of Barre has been placed in the city council room to replace a blue print map that had outgrown its usefulness. The map is enclosed in a frame of bird's eye maple and will be available for reference during the sessions of the council. It furnishes a complete guide to all city streets, private streets, railroads, streams, the ward lines and the city lines. It was prepared in the engineer's office and is one of a series to be distributed among the various city departments."

April 9, 1914: "George D. Morse of Worcester, Mass., arrived in the city this morning to install a number of new vending machines which he recently invented. The vendors are so constructed as to reject coins of a denomination larger than a penny or other metallic discs. Mr. Morse has had an interesting career and the patenting of the machine seems to have started him off on a lucrative business venture. When yet a young lad he peddled the *Worcester Evening Telegram* about the streets of his native city. Later he saved enough to send him through college and a few years since he ran on the Democratic ticket for an aldermanic office in Worcester. He was defeated but his opponent conceded him the largest Democratic vote ever polled to the ward. Outside of Boston and Worcester, Barre is the first town to have the machines installed."

June 4, 1914: "A considerable stir has been created in Barre over the practice of running automobiles through the city cemeteries. Almost everyone who has seen fit to join in the agitation has criticized the habit which some autoists have of guiding their cars around the cemeteries whenever occasion arises for going to the cemetery. Some people, and there are those who say they feel very keenly in the matter, point to the rule in other New England cities where the auto is inhibited from entering the burial grounds. According to those who are in a position to know, Elmwood cemetery is the more frequently visited of Barre's two larger graveyards. The question of putting a stop to the practice by creating a special ordinance for that purpose has been discussed several times."

August 5, 1914: "The Edison Diamond Disc phonograph agency is located at 94 North Main street, opposite Howland block. All are cordially invited to call and hear this new and wonderful instrument. Something entirely new, something different, something musical—a real achievement."

September 10, 1914: "A corn stalk, said to be the tallest ever seen in Barre, was brought from the Bolster farm in Barre Town and was seen by numerous passersby at the Bolster residence on North Main street. Not before this season has a stalk of corn been registered of such proportions. The stalk has been conspicuous on the farm for weeks past and only yesterday efforts were made to secure its accurate dimensions. The stalk measured exactly 12 feet and one inch in length."

October 15, 1914: "Work on the annex to the south end of the First Presbyterian church is to be resumed at once, according to a decision recently reached by the church governing board. It is planned to have the structure completed before cold weather begins and by the time it is finished an organ expert will be ready to install the pipe organ purchased by the church from St. Paul's church in Burlington several months ago. Building operations at the church were held up while a rearrangement of the floor space toward the front of the church was being made. Much of the organ is now in the church basement ready to be set up."

January 6, 1915: "Thus far the best results obtained by employes of the city water and fire departments in erecting skating rinks may be seen at Gospel Village, where one of the courts owned by the Barre Tennis club has been converted into a skating place that has attracted skaters old and young. There is another rink at the north end of the city and before the winter is very far advanced the city fathers hope to operate a rink at the Ayers street driving park." [Gospel Village is the current location of Lincoln House, formerly Lincoln Elementary School.]

February 8, 1915: "Police headquarters has received several complaints from people who claim to have been bothered by loiterers along North Main street. It is said that the practice of loafing in front of store and stairway entrances has become a real nuisance and the officers have been asked to disperse several knots of idlers gathered in the business section."

April 7, 1915: "Meadow Brook golfers, members of the club of that name, which has its course on the Brook street extension, have nearly completed their plans for the 1915 season on the links. The little structure which is serving the golfers as a clubhouse until more pretentious quarters can be provided, has been given a thorough overhauling and is in much better shape than formerly to accommodate the players. Arthur Pirie is president of the club and Donald McLeod was elected secretary at the last annual meeting. Several acquisitions to the membership are to be made before the season is in full swing. Since the middle of March a few of the most ardent devotees of the game have been pursuing the pastime on the course. Others swelled their number to-day when it was learned that the links, with the exception of the seventh green, are clear of snow and ice."

July 9, 1915: "After an absence of several weeks, in the course of which little children have been deprived of the privilege of squirting water upon

Rare interior view of Socialist Labor Hall with the children of Lawrence, Massachusetts strikers, Granite Street, February 1912. Note the framed Karl Marx pictures. *Aldrich Library Collection.*

each other on that particular corner of the park, the sanitary drinking fountain has been returned to the public square. The bubbler sent in its resignation one day and after that it refused to respond, either to the thirsty seeking an honest temperance drink or to the youngsters who are accustomed to use it as a plaything. The fountain has been repaired by the water department."

August 20, 1915: "Steel girders measuring 60 feet in length arrived in the city to-day and were transported immediately to the corner of Merchant and Main streets, where the Park Amusement Co. is erecting a new moving-picture and vaudeville theatre."

September 10, 1915: "Roderick Cameron, who has conducted a little grocery store at 171 Washington street for the past year, has work well under way on a new store building which he is to erect at the corner of Washington street and Huntington avenue. The excavation is being prepared for cement walls and the building will be two stories high, the first floor to be used for mercantile purposes and the second story as a dwelling for Mr. Cameron."

November 1, 1915: "Edward Blondin, who recently came to the Park theatre from the Grand theatre in Springfield, Mass., on the recommendation of the Powers company, began work to-day as a cinematograph operator at the local picture house. As a resident of Barre several years ago, Mr. Blondin served his apprenticeship in one of the theatres here, although he has since been employed in several large moving picture theatres in eastern cities."

January 5, 1916: "An unexpected rise in temperature has put a quietus on the plans of skating rink promoters in Barre and for the time being the hopes of many youngsters are sorrowfully blasted. The city street department is getting ready to assist in the building of rinks as soon as the weather conditions are suitable."

February 16, 1916: "Harry Broadwell, who is employed as a carpenter on the new station, which is being erected in Brattleboro, arrived in the city last evening for a few days' visit at his home on Mount street."

March 22, 1916: "When the time comes for furnishing each of Barre's licensed saloons with a posted list, there are some over 200 names that are to be proscribed before the moisture parlors are scarcely opened. City court records, dating from Nov. 1, 1915, are to contribute nearly

200 names of persons whose transgressions place them without the pale. Persons guilty of subsequent offenses or classed as habitual drunkards are to be posted along with the names of those who have been receiving assistance from the city."

April 10, 1916: "Benjamin Gasparello of 77 Franklin street returned to the city yesterday from New York, where he has been making a business visit of several days. During his absence, Mr. Gasparello closed negotiations for the purchase of 'Rinascenza Italia,' a weekly Italian newspaper published in Paterson, N.J. He will conduct the publication in connection with the weekly newspaper which he issues from his print shop on Merchant street, although the office and plant will remain in Paterson. Mr. Gasparello states that the Paterson publication, like the Barre weekly, is to be independent and strictly non-partisan."

July 15, 1916: "On the North Main street approach to Barre employes of the street department have set themselves to a commendable task in renewing stretches of highway that have been punctured with potholes for two seasons and more. From Jones Bros.' plant, north and south, quantities of stone are being dumped into the roadway and then rolled. The stone-crusher at Jones Bros.' is in almost constant operation during the work day."

September 20, 1916: "Another well known film concern is anxious to display Barre's famous granite industry on the screen and to the end that the pictures may be taken most advantageously, the general manager of the Town & Country Films, Inc., is corresponding with the secretary of the Granite Manufacturers' association. Sometime before snow flies the movie people plan to film the quarries as well as the cutting plants. It is represented that the educational film resulting from the cinematograph man's visit to the Barre granite region will be shown before 4,000,000 people in 3,000 theatres in the United States. Manufacturers and quarriers are going to co-operate with the picture folks."

November 21, 1916: "Contractor E.N. Philbrick, who is to erect a storage garage of considerable dimensions for H.F. Cutler on South Main street, is awaiting the arrival of a consignment of steel before beginning work on the structure. As soon as the material is on the grounds, the construction will be rushed forward as rapidly as possible. Mr. Cutler plans to have the building ready for occupancy in time to store a large number of automobiles for the winter."

Aldrich Public Library interior, probably around 1912. *Aldrich Library Collection.*

January 27, 1917: "An automobile with iron skids supplanting the forward wheels generously spiked with metal contrivances shot out of the Perry garage on Washington street this forenoon, took on Dr. J.A. Wark, and then swung up the hill to the east. Without the least hesitation, according to the operator, the hybrid Ford took the sharp pitches of Trow hill and completed an ascent that usually strikes terror to a good many motorists in the summer-time. Everywhere the driver and the doctor went the little machine did everything asked of it. Once back in the city, the autoist subjected the car to a stern test by heading it up Hooker hill and the results were wholly satisfactory. Ingenious repairmen at the garage have been contriving the device and with the completion of a successful test to-day they feel that they have solved one of the problems of winter motoring."

June 16, 1917: "The front outer wall of the old Methodist church on Church street has been renovated to the extent of a new coat of clapboards, and the carpenters have removed their standards to make way for painters. Some years ago the old church lost its tower because of growing dilapidation and uselessness. With the addition of the more recent repairs, the building has again become quite respectable as to outer appearance, and a coat of paint would make it almost like new." [The "old" Methodist church was moved to make room for the "new" church in the 1890s. Since then, it had been the site of various secular uses.]

September 8, 1917: "The street department has extended the new cement highway on North Main street to a point nearly even with the Berlin street intersection and by the end of next week the work will have been completed in every detail. Detour signs were removed several days ago and as rapidly as the cement squares hardened traffic has been diverted to the north and south instead of to the west by way of Smith street."

October 8, 1917: "Motorists whose travels carried them over the Montpelier road Saturday and Sunday are very forcible in their denunciation of conditions in the vicinity of Dodge's bridge, where mud holes created by highway builders rendered the roadway almost impassable. The character of the soil used in the construction work is condemned, as it was responsible for a deep slough into which automobiles slid easily, only to find that extrication was next to impossible. Motorists who examined the strata of building material used in the road say that every rain will make the strip impassable."

November 12, 1917: "Having purchased the laundry business of Charley Wong on Merchant street, I am prepared to turn out thorough workmanship at reasonable prices. Prompt service, three deliveries per week. William Young Wong, 10 Merchant street."

December 10, 1917: "The company which played 'Out There' before a small audience in the opera house Saturday evening, left yesterday for Claremont, N.H., where the players are booked for to-night. Arriving from Portland, Me., in one of the longest jumps on the circuit, the company was long overdue in reaching Barre. War taxes and a general policy of retrenchment which play-going people seem to be following appear to have wrought havoc with box office receipts, for members of the company reported poor houses along the line and at Portland, it was stated, the theatres are closed indefinitely. Manager Hoban of the local opera house has canceled a number of places which were booked for his theatre during and after the holiday season."

January 28, 1918: "Through A. Scampini, its agent, the Italian Athletic club has divided the Berlin street baseball park in lots and has disposed of some of the property already. Plans for a baseball team in 1918 are not maturing rapidly, and some doubt is expressed as to the possibilities of amateur or semi-professional baseball in Vermont this year. If a team is supported, its playing will probably be confined to Sunday baseball at Intercity park, and no Saturday schedule will be attempted." [As its name might suggest, Intercity Park was located between Barre and Montpelier. It was near the current Friendly's Restaurant.]

April 2, 1918: "George Jacobs, who has been identified with the livery business in Barre for many years, has leased the barn on South Main street vacated by James Gow, who is retiring from the livery business. Mr. Jacobs has reopened the stable for the accommodation of transients and for the purpose of boarding horses."

August 17, 1918: "Barre movie fans, who have been given a vacation from their favorite diversion during the past two weeks, are given a chance

View from Aldrich Library lawn about 1913. City Hall is to the left. *Aldrich Library Collection.*

to-day to once more see their favorite stars on the screen. During the past several days the Park theatre has been undergoing numerous repairs, while under the direction of Manager Mariani of the Bijou theatre, who recently vacated his quarters in the Arcade block, the Pavilion theatre on Pearl street will be reopened this afternoon, after remaining idle, as far as moving picture shows are concerned, during the past two years."

October 9, 1918: "North Main street pedestrians whose routes take them over Gunner brook at Blackwell street found that the necessity for crossing on the railroad or trolley trestles had passed to-day. This morning employes of the street department began the erection of a temporary footbridge to replace the bridge which the swollen waters of the stream washed away in the aftermath of the heavy rains Saturday night and Sunday. Work on the permanent structure which the department started a month ago is held up indefinitely and vehicular traffic continues to detour by way of North Seminary street, but it is the purpose of the street superintendent to cause pedestrians a minimum of inconvenience and to that end the temporary footbridge has been reconstructed as soon as possible."

December 18, 1918: "Again this winter the grounds in the rear of the Church street schoolhouse are to be used as a municipal woodyard, with the aldermanic charity committee in charge. It will not be a public wood market, as the supply to be unloaded there and worked into stove lengths will be used principally for the needs of the department. The first installment of wood consists of 200 cords, purchased a few days ago of a farmer living on the outskirts of the city. It will be hauled in the yard and sawed there within a few weeks. The committee purposes to erect temporary sheds for housing the supply."

March 22, 1919: "The U.S. employment bureau on North Main street was completely dismantled yesterday and closed its doors until sometime in the future if the government should appropriate the money to reopen it with the numerous others that have also closed. It is expected that the appropriation may possibly be made when Congress convenes in June and if such is the case, the smaller agencies that are being closed up at the present time will be reopened."

April 30, 1919: "The Vermont Fruit store, which has been in control of Fraquelli & Vanetti for several years, changed hands Monday. The purchaser is Antonio DePrato of Winooski. He has been associated with the Winooski Fruit Co. for the past ten years, so is well versed in the fruit business. Mr. Fraquelli expects to leave next week for Detroit, Mich. The other partner, Mr. Vanetti, died during the influenza epidemic last fall."

May 9, 1919: "The police department stationed the 'Keep to the Right' signs in the usual places this morning at the most traversed corners and thoroughfares, especially along Main street. All have been repainted a conspicuous bright red to be easily discerned by the drivers of all vehicles."

June 13, 1919: "The second issue of the *Spaulding Echo*, published for the benefit of the graduating students of the school as it contains the history of the class of 1919, was distributed to the students yesterday. As last year, every student of the class has a picture with a brief description of his high school life and characteristics displayed in school. One or two

Hotel Barre, around the time of its 1915 construction. Ten years later, a fifth floor was added. *Aldrich Library Collection.*

improvements, however, have been added and except for the changing of the color of blue and gold to green and gold of the cover, it is a duplicate of that published last year."

July 31, 1919: "O.H. Hale has rented the large store on Merchant street which adjoins his North Main street store, and by the removal of a partition has given much additional space to his store. Wide doors in the rear of the store on Merchant street will allow the receiving of automobiles, wagons, horses and other large pieces of property for sale."

October 1, 1919: "Workmen were engaged yesterday afternoon and this morning in tearing down the old Penniman house on South Main street, which is to be the site of the new Peerless Knitting Mills Co.'s $250,000 plant. This old edifice was one of the first houses to be built in Barre and comes apart comparatively easy. The wood and lumber will be sold on the spot and the debris cleared for action, as the work on the new building is soon to be started."

January 3, 1920: "Charles Barrows, the tailor, has installed in his shop over the Rogers shoe and clothing store, a new and costly steam pressing machine. It is a product of the United States Hoffman Machinery Co. and the latest model of its kind. Gas connections for heating purposes were made Wednesday afternoon. Mr. Barrows will no longer manipulate the 20-pound gas-heated flat iron which he has used for several years."

April 5, 1920: "Vandals were at work Saturday night and many broken panes of glass in the buildings in the north end of the city gave evidence of their work Sunday morning. In the building formerly known as Whitcomb Bros.' machine shop, now occupied by the Granite City garage and the Rae shoe shop, 17 panes of glass were broken out, while a little further to the north in the Henry Bosley paintshop the vandals punched out a plate glass window. Residents in a house just south of the garage building were awakened by something hurled against a window in their house at about midnight, and it is presumed that the glass-smashing attack in the other buildings was done at that time."

July 9, 1920: "A.S. Masi, proprietor of the small store at 36 South Main street, has begun the erection of a new store on a site near the present structure. On the lower floor he proposes to have his store and on the second floor a six-room tenement for his family."

August 28, 1920: "While driving his horse on North Main street Saturday afternoon, C. Pervasi of Williamstown found himself in a predicament when he tried to guide his horse and light wagon between an automobile parked at an angle and a street car. There wasn't room enough and the street car hit his left rear wheel and broke the hub somewhat. The driver was not thrown out although the wagon slanted in the collision. Mr. Pervasi complained about the practice of parking automobiles on Main street, especially when left at an angle, and said that the city ought not to allow it."

October 9, 1920: "The first vehicle crossed Jail branch over the new stone arch bridge on South Main street yesterday afternoon when the mayor drove his automobile across. In the car with the mayor were John Porter, Eddie Hall, Harold McAllister and Edw. Harlow, all of the bridge construction crew. They drove across going south, turned and returned. The bridge is not yet open to public travel, but it is expected it will be completed and open to the public about Nov. 1."

February 17, 1921: "E.O. Allen, who has disposed of his interest in the Allen Lumber Co. to the C.J. Allen estate, does not wish to have the impression go abroad that he is in poor health, as a statement in yesterday's paper made it appear. As a matter of fact, he is in good health and retired from the Allen Lumber company to engage in other work."

March 14, 1921: "Approximately two tons of rock dropped about 10 or 12 feet to the sidewalk from the Summer street ledge in front of Dr. Marshall Lamb's home sometime between Saturday night and early Sunday morning without doing damage to anyone or anything. The part of the ledge which dropped had protruded over the sidewalk, yet bore the appearance of being firm and safe for pedestrians to pass under, which hundreds did daily, including large numbers of little school children during the week days. Fortunately this mass of rock dropped to the ground and completely blocked the sidewalk when no one happened to be passing, probably in the early hours of Sunday morning after the heavy downfall of rain had reached the depth of frost."

July 15, 1921: "A.E. Massie, a South Main street merchant who with his family has occupied and conducted his business in the northern part of the old South End hotel building, has moved to his new home and business building at 36 South Main street. The building replaces an old

Left, Goddard Seminary graduate—and later Paramount Pictures film star—Miriam Hopkins with two friends, 1919. *Aldrich Library Collection.*

and much smaller structure, having ample store space on the ground floor and a six-room, well finished tenement on the second floor, which will be occupied by Mr. Massie's family. The erection of the building was started about a year ago soon after the old building was torn down, much of the work being done by Mr. Massie himself."

October 12, 1921: "A nice clean lot of high grade household furniture, including a dining room set, mahogany bedroom set, brass bed, rugs, dishes, etc., must be sold at sacrifice as we leave for California. Call Thursday or Friday. H.B. Blossom, 124 North Main street, over A.&P. store."

March 3, 1922: "The Drown Motor company of Barre has just opened a branch salesroom and office in Burlington, having quarters at 150 College street. This company has the state agency for the Velie and Earl cars and the northern Vermont agency for the Franklin."

May 13, 1922: "This city now has its second station equipped solely for the recharging and repair of storage batteries. This new shop has recently been opened up at 11 Granite street under the firm name of Milne & Nielson. George C. Milne and N. Nielson of this city are the proprietors of this new shop. Mr. Milne was until recently employed at the Oliver Battery station on North Main street and offers to give prompt, efficient and expert service on all types of batteries. The Yale battery will be on sale for every make of car as soon as a full complement has arrived."

June 15, 1922: "Barre is to have some swimming pools at last. Secretary Bradley of the Board of Trade stated this morning that if all those in the north end of the city interested in the building of a swimming pool would congregate near the brook behind the Marsh-Allen farm Friday and Saturday, armed with shovels and dressed for work, that the Board of Trade would have a team and scraper on hand to aid in digging out the brook and to construct a substantial dam. The young men and women in that section of the city have the kindness of the Marsh-Allen company to thank for offering the site to the Board of Trade free of all charge for the building of a swimming hole to be used by the public. The river in the rear of the McFarland farm on the road to South Barre has been sounded by President Carter and Secretary Bradley for the building of a swimming pool for the people in the south end of the city and it was found sufficiently deep. This pool could be put into excellent shape at a small cost to the board and will be done at once."

October 21, 1922: "Radio fans will no longer have to scour the country in order to purchase a receiving set, for the W.G. Reynolds company here has taken on the agency for handling a complete line of sets and parts for sets. Every variety of an instrument from the smaller and cheaper outfits to the large phone, equipped with a magnavox, is on display at the store. Mr. Reynolds was busy this morning having a set installed at the store and hoped to have it ready in time to get the Harvard-Centre game, play by play. It was found that a transformer was lacking and efforts were being made to locate one in time. The aerial for the office set which is of the same variety as recently gave a wonderful band concert on Boston Common, has been strung from the top of the Reynolds store to the chimney of the Bolster block the single variety being used for convenience. This outfit, known as a senior set, will pick up most of the more distant stations."

December 14, 1922: "The sound of the riveters' hammer has been ringing steadily in North Barre for the past few days while workmen for the Standard Oil company have been busy building one of the new large storage tanks on the company's West Second street lot."

January 6, 1923: "Questionnaires were being sent out this morning by Secretary Bradley of the Board of Trade to automobile owners, making an appeal for their aid in keeping the road between Barre and Montpelier open for motor traffic during the winter months. It is expected that there will be a generous response."

May 4, 1923: "Pole setters and linemen aided by a huge pole-placing outfit have been busy for the past week resetting old and putting in new poles along the northerly section of North Main street and they are gradually working their way southward."

June 13, 1923: "By laboring far into the early hours of the morning Chief of Police James Sullivan and Street Superintendent Witham swinging a paint brush, managed to complete the task of outlining the cross walks between the Park and Depot square with white paint. Motorists are asked to regard the new lines as a safety zone for pedestrians and they should remember that a pedestrian who steps into the street on one of these cross lanes has the right of way, so that if necessary the auto driver should stop. The police officials are out to see that the lines are regarded and there may be a few careless or heedless drivers brought into the station for a short visit before they can be made to realize that the pedestrian has any rights on the street."

July 10, 1923: "C.A. Heath, having purchased the Fifield block at 54–56 South Main street, is moving his stock of goods from 94 North Main street to the former named place, where, in addition to his line of wall paper, paints and varnishes, he will also carry a line of groceries, fruits, etc."

November 5, 1923: "Stores from Depot square to the Atlantic and Pacific store were plunged into darkness last Saturday evening during the rush hour shortly before 9 o'clock when a large transformer in front of the F.H. Rogers & Co. store went bad. Candles and gas had to be resorted to by the merchants who wished to carry on business, for it was well into the night before electricians had the break repaired."

February 12, 1924: "A rather novel form of winter sport has been originated by students at the Mathewson school, in pursuing which, no paraphernalia such as skis, snowshoes, sleds or jumpers, is necessary. Among the more advanced in the game, a thick sheet of wrapping paper is used, among the others, gravity and ice alone. The stunt is to slide down the twenty-foot sheet of glare ice which has formed on the embankment in front of the school and the less conventional the position in which the slide down is made, the higher the art of the slider."

April 26, 1924: "Elmer Hunting, for the past few years manager of the local Direct Importing Co. store, now the Cloverdale store, completes his duties to-night and Monday will take up the insurance work in Montpelier formerly done by Fred D. Kimball, who disappeared."

May 19, 1924: "The Vermont Transportation company started a second blue bus on the Burlington, Barre, Montpelier route Saturday afternoon, making, with the Yellow bus line's cars, well-nigh hourly service during the day between west state and east state."

June 9, 1924: "With perfect golfing weather, both local golf links, the Barre Golf club and the Meadowbrook club, were crowded to capacity

W.R. Cameron's grocery store, Washington Street, circa 1915. Cameron strove mightily to convince the Boy Scouts of America that Barre was its birthplace. *Vermont Historical Society.*

Saturday and Sunday by devotees of the tee and bunker. Many people also motored yesterday to the new country club links, where the work on the course is fast approaching completion."

August 9, 1924: "A growing business requires increased facilities and I am, therefore, moving from the L.M. Averill building into larger quarters over the W.D. Smith Co. store at 305 North Main street, formerly occupied by J.B. Kelly & Co. Beginning Aug. 11 I will be ready to serve you there with tailor-made clothing and expert repairing, cleaning and pressing for both ladies' and gents' clothing. Claude Druge."

October 4, 1924: "Quite a little favorable comment has been heard about the city during the past few days on the new signs marking the various main streets. For some time there has been an absence of markers and what remained were in such condition as to make them unreadable. The new signs were completed last week by George Reed and put into position by the street superintendent."

December 20, 1924: "The community Christmas tree, which is set up annually in the city park, was put up yesterday, and to-day electricians are busy wiring up the same with variously colored electric lights."

February 17, 1925: "The sprinkler system being installed in the city building by employes of the Rockwood Sprinkler company of Boston was completed this morning and given a preliminary test. It proved to work correctly. A gong has been installed on Prospect street to ring when one of the fire heads break and wires for another to be run to the fire station are being put up. The entire job will be completed by Thursday."

March 10, 1925: "The new city directories were distributed this morning and they are almost the same as those distributed last year. The cover color has been changed from red to pale blue and five more pages have been added so that the directory embracing Barre, Montpelier and nearby towns now contains 566 pages, making quite a sizable publication. The directories are printed by the H.A. Manning company of Springfield, Mass."

July 6, 1925: "A new building has been added at the tourist camp maintained at the trotting park by the Chamber of Commerce. A store has been erected and will be opened this week to sell groceries and commodities to campers."

August 17, 1925: "A little excitement was caused on North Main street yesterday about noon time when a gasket on a refrigerating machine in the basement of the creamery blew out and filled the building with ammonia, some of which escaped to the street."

December 2, 1925: "Going out of shoe business—We are closing out our shoes and overshoes at a wicked sacrifice, as we need out time to devote to our grocery business. Look us up for groceries and shoes, overshoes, rubbers, etc. L.E. Flint company store, 12 Church street."

January 2, 1926: "The huge searchlight which the Montpelier and Barre Light and Power company has been operating from the top of the Worthen building for advertising purposes was removed this morning."

February 25, 1926: "Several fire escapes were ordered to be installed on different buildings about the city last fall and up to date two have already been put on. G.L. Woodworth, proprietor of the Eastman block, has recently installed a fire escape on the west side of the building. A fire escape has also been installed on the west side of the Morse block, owned by C.W. Perry. Others are expected to follow suit soon. Although the city has been fortunate thus far this year in having few fires, and those of the chimney variety, Chief Heney wishes to warn against relinquishing the vigilance which has been kept up thus far against fires."

March 29, 1926: "Because Building Inspector George M. Rand refused to let the Barre Legion game with Montpelier Legion to-night be staged at the Church street gymnasium, on the ground that the building would not safely carry the large crowd that was expected, the local management arranged with the Barre school commissioners to hold the game at the Spaulding gymnasium instead."

May 11, 1926: "Workmen have been engaged for the past few days in remodeling a barn on West street on the property recently purchased by the A.W. Badger and company store. The barn is being converted into a modern four-car garage with a cement floor."

June 2, 1926: "A tourists' resort, known as 'The White House,' is fast nearing completion at the southerly end of South Main street on the premises of George E. McFarland. Already a new filling station has been erected with a building where soft drinks, candy and the like are being dispensed. The building is 12x24 feet and it is attractively painted in white and green. On each corner show windows have been placed where art goods to be sold are displayed. Inside the little building is varnished and painted. A counter has been set up where luncheons are to be served later. On each side of the gas and oil pumps there is a broad drive and next to the building a hollow has been filled in providing plenty of parking space. The McFarland home has also been repainted and decorated with an attractive sign, 'The White House,' displayed on the front lawn. With it is another sign making known to the motoring public that they can find rooms for the night if they wish. Just beyond the house a camp ground has been staked out for those who desire to pitch their tents beneath the stars. Electric lights are abundantly placed about the property making it doubly attractive at night. In the rear of the house, the old swimming pool that has been a favorite with boys and girls for years is also to undergo a metamorphosis. It is to be fixed up so that tourists may enjoy a comfortable bath in its cooling waters after a hard day's drive. The entire arrangement at the McFarland home is without a doubt the most attractive in this section of the state. At present the filling station and 'store' is in charge of Miss Ethel McFarland. Later she expects to devote her time to the sale of fancy work, novelties and pottery."

February 12, 1927: "The B.W. Hooker company has purchased a new combination motor ambulance and hearse, it having been delivered to them yesterday. The new hearse is of Cadillac make and is completely and moderately equipped. It is finished in dark gray and of exceptionally long

A disabled bus at 553 North Main Street (current site of People's Health and Wellness Clinic) in the aftermath of the flood of November 1927. *Vermont Historical Society.*

wheelbase. It will be added to the present equipment of the undertaking department of the firm."

March 22, 1927: "The property at 56 South Main street owned by the estate of Charles A. Heath has been sold to A. Popock of the Barre Dry Goods and Shoe store at 355 North Main street. After making alterations for a store he will remove his establishment from its present location to the newly-acquired building."

April 8, 1927: "The local police have received numerous complaints against speeding in the north and south ends of the city during the past few days. The biggest protest seems to come from the north-end where drivers start to step on the gas at Maple avenue and hit it up down along the new cement road. In the south-end the upper end of Main street and along the flat at the top of Jockey Hollow hill are rapidly becoming speedways. Motorists who do not heed this warning are liable to appear in court as numbers are to be taken and arrests made of speed artists."

June 9, 1927: "The street department has completed the work of laying one-half of the connecting link of pavement on Jockey Hollow hill, left last fall for the ground to settle. Within a few days that portion will be ready for use and work is already being started on the foundation for the left-hand strip."

July 12, 1927: "Among the local items in the *Barre Times* of July 12, 1898, a copy of which was sent to the *Times* office by Mrs. A.W. Clarke is the following: 'There was a heavy frost in this vicinity last evening and as a result the cucumber and tomato vines suffered.' The present month of July has had some cold days but none with frost sufficient to spoil cucumber and tomato vines. Another interesting item is the following: 'About 4000 people rode on the electric cars Sunday. Not a single day has passed yet that the road has not taken in $100 since it began running. Superintendent Smith has a gang of men at work repairing the tracks in several places, where they have been depressed by travel. Six cars are running now.' That, too, is somewhat different from this year."

November 14, 1927: "Conditions have improved so much in and around Barre that the pass system on the highways has been eliminated except on the East Montpelier and Montpelier roads for traffic going out of the city. Guards have been stationed for a week at the various approaches to the city and these will be removed except on the East

Montpelier and Montpelier roads, where outgoing traffic will be asked for passes."

December 2, 1927: "The Perry Automobile company, local agents for the Ford car, the new model of which had been advertised to be shown to-day, announced this morning that they were unable to get a car through at this time. They expect to have the new model on hand for display in about ten days."

Chapter 4

After the Flood and Through the War

1927–45

This era began just after the flood of November 3–4, 1927, visited devastation on Barre and many other Vermont communities. While the loss of life in Vermont did not approach the number of fatalities that were caused by the Mississippi River floods of the same year, many bridges and roads required considerable repair and replacement. Not long after 1927, the Great Depression hit the country and was followed, with little space between, by the United States' entrance into World War II.

While "Talk of the Town" continued its mission of providing much news of little import, its whimsicality and conversational tone were beginning to become less evident. A June 2, 1930 column shows, out of the twenty-six items, eighteen "comings and goings." Other items included one sick person, two births, one anniversary and one piece of club news. There was also an item about a poll taken of Barreites on the advisability of the repeal of Prohibition, a note about a recent fishermen's outing and a reminder about the upcoming dedication of a local airport.

January 23, 1928: "The Barre Auto Supply company which recently opened for business at 459 North Main street, has Robert Taylor, a local boy, as manager. Mr. Taylor has had over eight years' experience in the garage business, having been employed at the Perry Auto company and the Anderson garage. The store handles replacement parts to all cars but carries no accessories. It also is an official hydraulic brake service station."

February 2, 1928: "Skaters who have been complaining this winter because no rinks were provided because of the upset condition following the flood, have no further protest. At the side of the old North Barre rink at the corner of Third and North Main streets the fall rains covered a big area and it is now frozen over perfectly, forming as large a surface as youngsters have ever had to skate on there. The natural rink will hold dozens of skaters and a large number are taking advantage of the opportunity to enjoy the sport."

April 11, 1928: "More permanent crosswalk and parking markers are to be used by the city, small nickeled discs having been purchased that are to be set into cement in the street to do away with the unsatisfactory method of painting cross walks. Some of the discs are to be set to-day by the street department for a trial before all of them are put in."

July 2, 1928: "The balloon which was tied to a pump at the Kirk and Gibb filling station, met an untimely end yesterday, when it was cut from its moorings by some men traveling in a Lincoln car which bore a Massachusetts number plate. The balloon burst while in the air. George Tucker found the pieces in Graniteville."

October 13, 1928: "The Green Mountain Power company had its employes at work installing two new street lights on Pearl street this morning. Foundations for the lights had been put in some time ago but work of putting up the fixtures was delayed until after the work of paving the street was completed. The two new street lights will be the first on Pearl street since it was built and will be a decided improvement."

December 22, 1928: "Dr. Jarvis and his little symphony orchestra added a tuneful touch to the Christmas season last night when they played carols from the bandstand in the city park at the rear of the beautifully lighted Christmas tree recently put up by the lighting company. The youngsters in the band braved the cold of the night for over an hour before they adjourned to the armory to play at the Spaulding game."

May 14, 1929: "The police department was engaged to-day in putting up signs at the various entrances to the city indicating to visiting motorists that the speed limit in the city is 20 miles per hour. The signs are attractively printed and easily legible. The police department is to start a campaign against city speeders at once."

June 21, 1929: "The fire department made a test run last evening about 7:30 o'clock to try out the second sirene which has just been installed on North Main street. The warning signal has been placed at the corner of Merchant street and Main. During the test last evening, with both of the sirenes working, the apparatus was able to get to North Seminary street before the warning stopped wailing. Motorists are responding well to the signals, pulling their cars clear of the street and remaining stopped until the trucks pass."

July 20, 1929: "No left turns are to be permitted off Main street and going into Keith avenue hereafter. A small plate was attached to the traffic beacon at the intersection of the two streets last evening giving motorists warning that they are not to turn left at that point. Left turns have resulted in a great confusion and delay of traffic."

August 17, 1929: "Chief of Police James Sullivan has received a number of complaints that bathers are leaving the gateway open on the Tucker property near the new swimming pool with the result that cows pastured on the property are getting out. Bathers are asked to make certain that all gates are closed behind them as they go to and from the pool."

The B. Tomasi Block, circa 1930. This building stood near where the Soup N' Greens Restaurant is currently located. *Aldrich Library Collection.*

September 7, 1929: "There is being built at the police station a granite slab driveway into the basement. The old dirt driveway was causing considerable bother when it rained by letting mud and sand into the basement."

November 2, 1929: "The D.A. Perry Real Estate agency has sold four lots of land on Autocrest, the plot opposite the Jones Brothers' granite plant on the Montpelier road. The lots known as the Belville property were purchased by Mr. and Mrs. Leonard R. Muckler of this city, who buy for investment purposes."

March 6, 1930: "The city court chamber, which for the past few years has been gradually becoming so dingy and dark that the color in which it was originally decorated can be only a matter of conjecture, is undergoing a renovating process. A group of painters, decorators and repair men started at work this morning, transforming the interior of the place, and in a few days it should present a much more gratifying appearance."

May 8, 1930: "Interest is running high in the new Tom Thumb golf course on South Main street and both yesterday and to-day a large number of people appeared to try it out. The installation of flood lights was completed to-day and Messrs. Gomo and Grady plan to have their formal opening to-night. At that time Ollie Brault, professional at the local Country club, will engage in a match against the Montpelier Country club professional. The match is slated for 8 o'clock. The greens at the course have been the subject of much interest. They are made from cotton seed hulls dyed and rolled."

September 6, 1930: "One local lovers' lane is being demolished in the breaking up of the wooded park between Currier and Camp streets, which was sold recently by M.H. McAllister to a real estate dealer in Hardwick, who is planning the development of that section into city streets."

November 7, 1930: "The audience was alarmed last night at the Park theatre when one of the vaudeville cast fell hard during a roller skate act in which she was twirled about in the air clinging to her partner's neck by her toes. The same act was performed a second time with no accident, and the audience applauded heartily."

December 4, 1930: "The colored lights to decorate the business section of Barre have been strung across the street in several places, from the Peoples National bank as far north as Granite street, ready for the lighting."

February 16, 1931: "The Green Mountain Stationery Company, Inc., of Barre, incorporated by Gladys H. Cheyne, Lester J. Cheyne and Neale W. Hooker of Barre, to sell stationery, office supplies and machines with a capital stock of $10,000 has filed its articles of association in the secretary of state's office in Montpelier."

March 2, 1931: "Harry Levin of 20 Park street entered the Harvard Clothing store at 315 North Main this morning as manager of the store, and hopes to meet his old customers there. Mr. Levin just concluded his services for the Montgomery Ward company, having been manager of the clothing department in their local store since it opened here 13 months ago."

May 20, 1931: "The Spencer Sign Service shop which was recently burned out in its location near the Park theatre, is to be reopened at once in the Central House block on Pearl street. The store recently used as a Franklin show room is being remodeled to be used for a shop by Mr. Spencer."

June 30, 1931: "The Knights of Columbus in Barre will be at home soon in newly arranged rooms at the location over the Grand Union store that was the barber shop formerly owned by Andrew Mylnarchik, and later by Albert Ponton. Archie Adams and employes are refurnishing the rooms and making the place suitable for club headquarters. The Knights of Columbus recently sold their home at the corner of Merchant and Summer streets."

July 7, 1931: "Men of Main street laughed again today with Henry Lundy, their negro friend who has come back to Barre after passing four years in St. Petersburg, Va. He was busy this morning shaking hands with a host of old friends and acquaintances who think the depression is over now that 'Bud' has come back home."

August 8, 1931: "The city street department commenced work yesterday pouring the cement for the new curb, gutter and sidewalk on the easterly side of Washington street from the end of the present walk to Charles street."

December 8, 1931: "The swimming pool at the Recreation field is to be kept cleared this winter for a skating rink and lights are to be put up there so that skating can be enjoyed at night."

February 12, 1932: "John McKay, general manager of the New England division of the Cloverdale stores, returned last evening to Boston after having come to Barre for the opening of the remodeled store of that company in this city. Mr. McKay stated yesterday when interrogated as to how general business conditions effected the stores in his division, stated that business was below normal. In some sections of New England the depression appeared more evident than in others and while the business in many of the 60 Vermont stores has fallen off considerably, this store does not appear to be as badly hit as some of the others. Mr. McKay was highly pleased with the interest shown in the store here yesterday and commented on the unusually heavy business done. Other district men who came here for the opening also returned yesterday to their respective divisions and Miss Mary Morrison, chief dietitian of the Cloverdale stores, returned to Boston. Miss Morrison, who has recently returned from a visit to the government food laboratories in Washington and the Good Housekeeping Institute, gave a large number of Barre women some interesting information yesterday on the subject of cooking meats. She has been making a special study of that subject for some months."

March 5, 1932: "Lane Construction company men have just completed remodeling a section of the M.H. Fishman store, and a dress department with full lines of dresses has been added. The new department is in charge of Miss Jessie McAllan."

April 19, 1932: "The Church street numbering of houses, officially changed several months ago but not changed on residences until very recently, has caused some little confusion on that street. New numbers placed at the former 26 and 28 are now 176 and 178, whereas across the street the numbers remain 22 and 24. The change was instituted when confusion resulted because the first few numbers appeared on the street twice, beginning at the corner of Prospect and South Main streets, and again at the crossing of Church and Washington streets."

May 19, 1932: "The town clock is stopped and city officials have become very much aware of it, having had numerous calls from people who desired to call their attention to it. The clock is out of order and repairs on it will be necessary before it can again give Barre people an idea of the correct time." [The town clock is still located on the Universalist church steeple.]

June 16, 1932: "Very few people have a real conception of the number of men who are wandering about the country, many of them in search

J. Leo Messier and his Symphonic Dance Orchestra, Barre Opera House, 1933. *Aldrich Library Collection.*

of employment. The records at the police station kept of lodgers, shows that since January 16 of this year a total of 489 men have been given lodging and at times there were eight and ten men bunked at the station on the same night. Only six nights passed without any lodgers at all since that time."

November 17, 1932: "The first hole-in-one was registered on the new Barre Golf club links last week when Douglas Newcombe played the short eight hole on the course in a single stroke. Most of the other courses in the city have had several aces registered on various holes but the one scored by Newcombe was the first on the new course opened up only two years ago. It was probably the first hole in one scored in November in Vermont when the golf season is usually long since closed."

January 14, 1933: "The 'municipal club room' in the basement of the city hall next to the room used by the city band, was opened up this week and has not proved really popular yet as a meeting place for unemployed men. On cold days the 'members' of the club congregate there but they prefer to remain outside on warmer days."

March 21, 1933: "A meeting of the sisterhood of the Congregation Thihereth Mosha was held Monday evening at their rooms in the Currier block. After the regular meeting a cultural program followed during which the present situation in Germany was seriously discussed. The members officially registered their protest against the Hitler anti-Semitic atrocities. This protocol was sent to the committee of One Hundred in New York city, who is taking definite steps in voicing the sentiment of the American public against discrimination of Jews in Germany."

May 2, 1933: "The sale of beer by second class licensees was fairly steady all day yesterday with grocery establishments doing the heavy volume of case businesses. Many people are reported holding off on their orders for the 3.2 brew until other varieties arrive here. First class establishments had a light sale during the day but last evening they did a rushing business, the warm night providing ideal conditions for serving the beer." [This event marked the end of Prohibition in Barre.]

July 14, 1933: "Two members of the veteran's C.C.C. camp at East Barre were picked up on North Main street last night by the local police after they had been imbibing too freely of rubbing alcohol and had decided to go to sleep in front of the Miles block on the sidewalk. They were detained at the police station for the night and this morning, after arrangements had been made for their punishment, Captain Savage had them taken to the Kimball Corner camp."

October 13, 1933: "Anthony Tomasi not only complies with the NRA, but how he complies! You will remember that old big brown eagle he sticks out in the front window of his cash market every few weeks just to attract attention, or something. Well that eagle, which first was displayed before Roosevelt was born, as it has been estimated, is now a blue eagle. His feathers have all taken on a new hue, and he flocks proudly with the eagles on the NRA stickers in the Tomasi store windows, and the Symbolic bird enjoys it so much that he sits up 30 per cent straighter in his new raiment. This morning a few Democrats were trying to get him to talk by calling him Delano."

February 14, 1934: "A French Mardi gras last night at the Hollywood café attracted a crowd estimated at more than 200 persons, the majority of whom were members of the St. Jean Baptiste society of Barre. The president of that society, William Provencher, sponsored the event, and invited numerous guests from Montpelier and surrounding towns. Dancing was from 8:30 to 12 o'clock, the Bar-X cowboys of St. Johnsbury furnishing musical inspiration. When announcements of the best costumes were made, those receiving distinction were Mr. and Mrs. John Fugere, who came as Liberty and Uncle Sam. Booby prizes were awarded Louis Gagne and Mrs. J. Rene LaRouche, for their costumes representing an old lady and Topsy, respectively."

June 18, 1934: "Barre's new liquor store under state control opened this morning on Elm street with Peter Hamel as manager and James C. Johnston as assistant. A full stock of assorted liquors has been received and placed in the establishment. Under the terms of the new liquor law, the store is not permitted to do advertising of any sort other than to hand price lists to customers visiting the store. An ample supply of the lists have been received for distribution."

July 26, 1934: "The Carle-Belville company is employing six men remodeling the front of the Lane building at the corner of Seminary and North Main street, where a filling station and store is to be constructed. Ernest Belville stated this morning there will be two entrances to the place, one to the gasoline pumps and one to the store, and that it is expected the work will be completed within a month. The firm will not vacate its present quarters in the adjoining building on North Main street, but will use that space as well as the additional place."

November 17, 1934: "The last of the cement was poured into the new sidewalk on the north side of Depot square yesterday afternoon and by Monday will be ready to walk upon."

December 11, 1934: "Harley DeCoteau of Montpelier had a narrow escape from injury in front of the city hall here yesterday afternoon. DeCoteau started to crank a Chevrolet car, in which his mother, Mrs. G.J. DeCoteau, was sitting. The car, unknown to the boy, was in high gear. When he turned the crank over, the engine suddenly fired and the car started ahead and jumped the curbing. The boy jumped out of the way, the car narrowly missing pinning him as it crossed the sidewalk and smashed up against the granite front of the building. Fortunately, there was no one in the path of the car. The bumper of the automobile was smashed off in striking the building with considerable force and Mrs. DeCoteau suffered a wrenched neck."

January 4, 1935: "B.W. Hooker & company yesterday completed the removal of burial caskets and undertaking equipment from the quarters which they have occupied for many years on the second floor of the Blanchard block, to their funeral home on Academy street which is rapidly nearing completion. Workmen are still employed at the funeral home but within a short time it will be finished and ready for inspection."

April 30, 1935: "The Barre restaurant is undergoing alterations and repairs at the hands of a group of restaurant specialists. New toilet facilities are being installed to comply with the regulations of the state liquor board and the proprietor, Arthur Canatselos, plans to have the entire interior of the establishment gone over in a new color scheme."

May 3, 1935: "Cab Calloway and his famous colored orchestra which played at Burlington earlier this week, stopped at the Central Hotel last night. They have been filling several engagements in Vermont and New Hampshire."

June 4, 1935: "Men who enjoy sitting in the city park during the summer afternoons have been complaining because of the fact that the drinking bubblers at the park are not yet in operation. The warm weather of the past few days has driven many people to the bubblers in anticipation of a cooling drink but were all disappointed for neither of the drinking fountains have been turned on as yet."

September 6, 1935: "The Midway Golf club members, 50 strong, ate roast corn, 'hot dogs' and marshmallows last evening at a roast held on the clubhouse 'lawn.' The event, while not marking the close of the season in a way denoted the added activity at the club this summer, an activity that is continuing daily, although the club tournament has been played. Members chipped in for the provender they consumed."

October 2, 1935: "Attention of the street department was called yesterday to the fact that quite a number of street signs are missing about the city. The aluminum signs now in use are easily broken and on Washington street alone several signs marking side streets are missing. The absence of street markings makes it difficult for strangers to find their way about Barre quickly and the department plans to take immediate steps to see that all signs are replaced."

February 11, 1936: "A.B. Lane, local contractor, started a gang of men this morning on the job of remodeling the Green Mountain diner. Plans call for enlarging the kitchen of the diner, extending counters to a much greater length and the construction of several new dining booths."

March 9, 1936: "Avenire Fracassi is the first in Barre to install one of the new AGA stoves, a recent Swedish invention, made by a blind man whose scientific advances won the Nobel prize. The stove Mr. Fracassi installed in his restaurant at 405 North Main street is a large three-griddle stove. The insulation of the fire box makes it possible to touch the outer part of the stove without burning the fingers, while the griddles, covered when not in use, are ever hot. Mr. Fracassi illustrated the power of the stove this morning by placing a pan with cold water on the first griddle. The water, an inch deep in the pan, came to a boil in 40 seconds."

May 12, 1936: "The old wood-working shop located on the lot at the rear of the Barre Steam laundry between North Main and Summer streets, will soon be no more. The rambling old shop has been a familiar landmark for many years and it came in for lots of attention some years ago at the time of the Broadwell murder case when the body of Mrs. Broadwell was found near the Main street end of the building. The shop was operated by a number of different concerns in recent years and lately had been known as the Rowell and Flint shop, being operated up until a few months ago. For the past day or two a group of workmen have been engaged on the task of razing the old building."

October 2, 1936: "Police officer William Daniels was called to the M.H. Fishman store this morning about 11 o'clock when it was discovered that there was a small calibre bullet hole through one of the front windows on the northerly end of the store. The officer found a .22 shell outside the window, the shell having been exploded. Store officials did not know when the hole was made in the window. A more complete investigation of the matter is to be made."

November 12, 1936: "A set of round metal plates have been set into the pavement around the traffic beacons just north of the city park. Some trouble has been experienced by the police with out-of-state cars going south on Main street, cutting in between the two beacons in making a turn up Washington street and the new discs which are to be given a coat of paint, are expected to guide traffic in the proper line around the beacons."

December 5, 1936: "Work has been started on the new hockey rink to be built at the rear of the North Barre skating rink near Fourth street. Six men were given work clearing snow, cutting brush, and preparing the area for leveling. The work is being pushed along as rapidly as possible under the existing weather conditions in order that the new rink may be ready for use this month. Yesterday police posted warning signs in that area both for the protection of skaters crossing the highway and to protect children sliding on Third street which has been opened this year for coasting."

January 7, 1937: "Police this morning discovered an act of vandalism committed some time last night at the bandstand in the city park. Three of the light shades had been torn down and cast out into the street with the sockets ripped off the wires and several light bulbs missing. An investigation was being made today to try to determine who was responsible for the offense."

March 6, 1937: "Bullets were flying yesterday in a battery recharging building near the Central Vermont station. A youngster tossed half a box of .22 calibre ammunition into a store in the building and before long the bullets began to pop. The boy suffered a slight burn on one hand and the store was somewhat ventilated but no great damage was done. Police were called to make an investigation of the incident."

May 18, 1937: "Work is progressing rapidly on the store in the Blanchard block to be occupied by the J.C. Penney company. Painters are already at work on the interior of the store and workmen are engaged in putting in the front panel work. Some trouble was experienced with youngsters marking initials in the fresh plastering on the front of the building until a foreman discovered the boy responsible for trying to inscribe his initials for posterity to see, and gave the youngster a warning which stopped the practice."

September 8, 1937: "Workmen started yesterday the task of erecting a new marquee in front of the Barre opera house. It is expected that the task will require about a week to complete. Sound engineers from the Western Electric company also started today on the job of installing new sound equipment in the theatre. The theatre remains open while the work is in progress."

January 4, 1938: "Police records compiled today indicated that 568 men were given lodging overnight in the cell room during the past year.

Damage on Church Street from the hurricane of September 21, 1938. *Aldrich Library Collection.*

November was the high month, when a total of 80 men applied for a bed for the night, and the monthly average was slightly over 47 men."

February 19, 1938: "Notice was received yesterday by Manager Louis Stern of the Barre opera house from State's Attorney Webster E. Miller that Sunday movies be discontinued. Mr. Stern stated that he was informed that after tomorrow's shows he would not be permitted to operate on Sunday. All local theatres have been running Sunday shows in recent weeks. Manager John Hassett of the Paramount theatre stated today that he had not received notice from his home office that shows must be discontinued on Sunday and will show tomorrow as usual. The Magnet theatre also had a Sunday picture planned for tomorrow." [Communities were no longer forbidden by the state to have Sunday movies, beginning in 1939.]

May 7, 1938: "Police have been engaged for some time in investigating reports that marihuana cigarettes, often termed 'reefers,' are being sold in this city. Rumors have been current about the city for some time that the doped cigarettes with the Mexican weed which distorts mental workings are being peddled here. Other cities in the country have had considerable trouble with the doped cigarettes being peddled among youngsters of high school age. Chief of Police Donahue admitted this morning that the matter has come to the attention of his department but there are no developments in the investigation as yet."

July 30, 1938: "Police were seeking today to learn some of the details of a fight which took place last evening in front of the Silver Top tavern on North Main street. Unofficial reports were that six or eight men were involved in the affray and the sidewalk in that section was blood-spattered this morning."

September 9, 1938: "The picket who has been stationed in front of the Lafayette and Ross barber shops for a few weeks is now engaged in picketing work in front of other non-union shops. Today he is pacing back and forth in front of the Poulin Brothers' barber shop at 10 Merchant street."

December 21, 1938: "Officials of the Burlington Building & Wrecking company arrived in this city yesterday to sign final contracts and fix up other matters in connection with the razing of the Goddard school property. They started work on the actual razing operation today and the old barn and gymnasium will come down first to enable the wreckers to use the material for fencing off the main school building while it is being torn down."

January 17, 1939: "The north face of the town clock made a very presentable appearance this morning, it having been fitted with a new pair of hands to replace those which broke off a few days ago. The shiny hands are in decided contrast to the old ones on the other clock faces. Today none of the faces of the clock was giving anything approaching the correct time."

March 16, 1939: "Painters have completed the task of renovating and redecorating the opera house corridors and stairways which were covered with water stains and dirt from a recent fire in the attic of the city hall building. Repairs have also been made to the Ladies of the G.A.R. room which was damaged at the same time."

June 8, 1939: "The set-up of the local Coca-Cola bottling firm was explained yesterday to Rotarians by Henry Miller, plant manager, and Hal Miller, sales manager. The firm is an authorized Vermont corporation and it hires all Vermont labor. It purchases its syrup from the Coca-Cola organizations with which it has a franchise to distribute the product in northeastern Vermont. The local plant is located on North Main street in the place formerly occupied by the Perry Automobile Co. garage. The program was in charge of Lester J. Cheyne."

August 9, 1939: "The city council will make an official inspection of the new municipal auditorium project tonight at 5 o'clock with Architect William Freeman of Burlington. The project is now at its most interesting stage and the construction of the building can be appreciated before it is closed in."

September 29, 1939: "The Haskett Sport shop has been undergoing some remodeling this week. A partition at the rear of the store has been moved out, adding a number of feet to the store proper. The rear of the establishment is being fitted up as a gun and ammunition department for better service to local sportsmen. The added space will permit showing a more diversified line of sporting goods in the future."

October 9, 1939: "Police were called this morning to the Granite City Auto Sales Co. yard at the corner of North Main and West streets. Sometime over the week end thieves, probably youths, went through the used car lot at the garage headquarters and stripped cars of shifting lever tops, ash trays and other accessories. Officer Robert Leslie investigated the case."

January 4, 1940: "The Quality Grocery at 161 Washington street, owned by Patrick McGuire, has been purchased by Louis Ziter, who has taken immediate possession. Mr. Ziter is putting in a complete line of fresh staple groceries, meats and provisions and expects to give good service, including free delivery."

March 8, 1940: "Police have been experiencing some trouble with the automatic control on the city traffic lights this week. This morning for the second time the lights stuck on one color. Earlier in the week the red light stuck for some minutes before the difficulty was noticed and traffic piled up. As soon as drivers realized that the lights were stuck traffic resumed and a power company employe removed the difficulty. Today the trouble was discovered and remedied in short order."

April 26, 1940: "The B.W. Hooker & Co. furniture store started construction yesterday on the new building which the concern will occupy north of the Clarence A. Dodge home on the Montpelier road. The new building is to be of wood construction and it will be about 100 by 100 feet, one story high. The architect on the building is Charles Helmer of Chelsea and the construction work is being done by the A.B. Lane contracting firm of this city. The building will be completed during the coming month of May and it will be occupied by the Hooker company upon completion."

May 4, 1940: "Work on the long-awaited project of resurfacing Main street started today. Assistant City Engineer John D. Cook with his assistants, Frank L. Tucker and Elwin Martin, were busy at an early hour taking measurements and grades. The proposed project will include the Main street section between the People's National bank and Keith avenue."

June 7, 1940: "The Main street paving project, being carried on under a WPA program, which has been proceeding rapidly, was nearing completion this morning. Before noon today the final strip of cement was in and workmen have only the gutter to put in on the westerly side of the street to complete the paving from Elm street to Keith avenue. The smoothness of the new surface, as compared with the old granite block pavement, is already being appreciated with only half the street open."

October 11, 1940: "Melvin Peabody returned today to his work as a musician at the Mountain View house at Whitefield, N.H. A five-pound son, Melvin Allen, was born yesterday at the Barre City hospital to Mr. and Mrs. Peabody."

December 7, 1940: "Edward Milne of Graniteville narrowly escaped a bad accident about 3 o'clock this morning near the intersection of Wellington and Merchant streets. He was driving down Merchant street when a car shot out of Wellington street. In trying to avoid it he went over the sidewalk and against a rather flimsy iron guard railing at the edge of a steep embankment. The cars did not collide and the guard rail held enough to prevent the Milne car from going over the bank although some damage was done to both the car and the railing. Police were notified of the accident."

January 13, 1941: "Four cars were involved in an accident which happened at 4:30 o'clock yesterday afternoon near the Washington street traffic beacon. A car, operated by Arnold Sinclair of this city, stopped for a red light. A car, operated by Hazel Pittsley of South Barre, following

Interior of Barre Municipal Auditorium, July 1941. *Aldrich Library Collection.*

the Sinclair car, was unable to stop on the icy highway and rammed the Sinclair car from the rear. Still a third car, operated by Murdine Thurston of Montpelier, rammed the rear of the Pittsley car and a moment later a fourth car, operated by Charlotte Hartwell of Montpelier, bumped the rear of the Thurston car. Fenders, bumpers and grills were damaged in the multiple collision. Officer Edward O'Connor investigated the accident."

April 15, 1941: "Miss Helen Cate of 40 Perry street, art supervisor in the local public school system, is passing the spring recess at her home in Marblehead, Mass."

May 5, 1941: "The University of Vermont band was in Barre Saturday afternoon during the course of a two-day tour through parts of Vermont. The band unlimbered on the south side of the city park and then paraded through some of the streets of the city. The music and the snappy marching were much enjoyed by a large number of people."

July 8, 1941: "A rain which began with thunder showers early last evening and continued throughout most of the night and early morning was welcomed by local gardeners and farmers whose fields and gardens

South Main Street, Trow and Holden, circa 1942. *Aldrich Library Collection.*

were rather dry. The rain also served to raise some of the streams which were very low. The rain was so heavy that it did some damage by washing out cold patch on hill streets as the water came too fast for receivers to carry it off. Grading about some of the new homes in the city also suffered from the heavy downpour which washed out loosely packed lawns."

August 6, 1941: "Mrs. Angel Gomez and Mr. and Mrs. Manuel Pena and child of Detroit, are visiting at the home of Mrs. Chester Meaker of North Main street."

September 12, 1941: "Leo Young of Orange has returned to his home after having been employed for several months in Bermuda on a naval base project. Young, who was employed as a guard, returned home because of a fever which incapacitated him. He reported that a number of Barre Town men are returning this weekend from Bermuda because of their inability to stand conditions there. The lack of good water and the quality of food, Young said, were the chief complaints, but he said that the excessive heat and homesickness of the men was the real reason for most of them leaving the high wages to be obtained there. Young said that the minimum pay was $66 a week on the project."

January 14, 1942: "Overseer of the Poor Nellie Balich reported this morning that the new A&P supermarket had donated about 1,000 loaves of bread to her department, together with a number of doughnuts and frankfort rolls. These will be given out this afternoon from the overseer's office in city hall. The needy who wish a supply should call at once, and are requested to bring their own containers."

April 7, 1942: "Dog owners are becoming very much alarmed over an epidemic which appears to be some new form of distemper sweeping through animals in this area. Yesterday another local man lost a valuable dog, this time a cocker spaniel. Numerous other dogs are reported ill and several dog owners over the week end dispatched pets which developed a paralysis of the rear legs. Cats are also succumbing to the same disease. Altogether more than two dozen valuable animals, valuable at least to their owners, have died in recent weeks. So far as is known no analysis of any of the animals has been completed to determine the exact cause of the epidemic."

May 5, 1942: "The first group of women in this vicinity to learn machine tool operation started their training period yesterday at the NYA resident training center at Waterbury. Nine Barre women were in the first group, although it is expected further assignments will be made this week. The women return home each night, transportation being furnished. They receive $24.80 a month while learning. Any girl between 17 and 24 interested in such training could contact the Barre office of the United States employment office. Barre women who started the course yesterday were Mary P. Carpenter, Josephine Saliba, Tomasa Moruzzi, Lorraine White, Marilyn Schoff, Annie Masi, Genora Foiadelli, Nellie French and Theresa Habbep."

June 9, 1942: "Tax Collector Guy J. Dindo issued warning today that a person applying for an operator's license must not falsify his or her declaration on the operator's license application by certifying that his (or her) poll taxes have been paid, when such is not the case. Section 5090 of the public laws of Vermont provides for suspension of the operator's license of any person who fails to pay all poll and old age assistance taxes for which he is liable. This includes the taxes of the wife of such a person."

January 9, 1943: "The surprise blackout last night held no terror for the Girl Scouts, troop six, who were caught at the close of their meeting. They remained till the all-clear signal, singing, telling jokes and presenting riddles. Esperanza Canizo sang several solos, one of which was very appropriate, being entitled: 'When the Lights Come On Again.' During the meeting the girls voted to have a play which will be given later."

March 16, 1943: "Mrs. Harry C. Mackenzie has gone to Alamogordo, N.M., to visit her husband, Sergeant Mackenzie, who is stationed at the army base there. She will spend a month there. En route she visited Sergt. J. Wendell Mackenzie, who is stationed in Chicago. The sergeants are brothers."

April 6, 1943: "Ralph Caccavo returned today to his studies at Tufts college, Medford, Mass., after passing a vacation with relatives here and

Parade on Washington Street, July 26, 1942. *Fred Pirie photo.*

in Northfield. He was accompanied by his roommate, Donald C. Abbey, who has been passing several days here."

May 1, 1943: "Rationing came to Elm street yesterday and it has nothing to do with sugar, shoes or sirloin. Customers calling at the state liquor store were told that hereafter purchasers must restrict the purchase of a favored beverage to two bottles. Liquor rationing is already a wartime measure in Canada and a number of western states have limited alcoholic purchases for several months. Short liquor rations to Vermont became effective only this week and it has been intimated that more drastic curtailments may be ahead."

June 5, 1943: "Rino Lasorsa has completed his first year studies at the University of Illinois in Champaign, and has returned to his home on Ayers street to await his call to military service."

July 15, 1943: "In these days when there is a priority rating for the purchase of bicycles, local bicycle owners seem to be surprisingly careless in leaving their bicycles around. Police last night picked up two more bicycles apparently abandoned on Main street and took them to the station. This brings the total of bicycles at the police station to three picked up within the last few days."

September 3, 1943: "Barre boys and girls between 12 and 16 years of age can fight on the home front by helping tomorrow at the victory carnival. These patriotic helpers of the service men and women in the district are asked to attend a meeting at 7 o'clock this evening in the city court room where they will receive their instructions."

February 17, 1944: "Two Barre boys, members of a youthful gang which had made a large number of breaks into local business establishments, were arraigned in Barre juvenile court this morning. A 15-year-old boy was adjudged to be a delinquent and Judge H. William Scott ordered him to be committed to Weeks school until he becomes 18 years old, which will be Nov. 11, 1946. This youth was involved in the breaks made at night at the Barquin store on North Main street and the Central market on Summer street and from other places. The other boy, 13 years old, was also adjudged delinquent, and he was paroled in custody of his parents pending sentence and further orders. The boy allegedly stole $2 from the American Oil station, 50¢ from Forger's Gulf Service station and made breaks into the Esso Filling station, I. John's Filling station and McLeod's blacksmith shop."

March 16, 1944: "One of the largest girl babies to be born at Barre City hospital for some time was the nine and one-half pound daughter born this morning to Mr. and Mrs. Americo Gioria of Websterville."

April 3, 1944: "Mrs. Oreste Valsangiacomo has returned to the Maple avenue home of her mother, Mrs. Anna M. Emslie from the Heaton hospital, Montpelier, where she underwent an appendectomy."

June 6, 1944: "Announcement was made today of the purchase by B.W. Hooker company of the repair shop on Pearl street operated and owned for some five years by Charles Chiarvalli of 108 Summer street. Mr. Chiarvalli framed pictures, fixed shades, did upholstery work, rug binding and other odd jobs of similar nature. The company bought all the equipment and material in the shop which will be closed. Mr. Chiarvalli will now be employed by Hooker's, and he will do the same type of work with the exception of upholstery work. Before opening his shop on Pearl street, he was employed about 35 years by the Hooker company."

July 8, 1944: "Mr. and Mrs. Max A. Holden of Washington street have returned to their camp at Highgate Springs after spending a few days at their home here. Mr. Holden will return here tomorrow night."

August 16, 1944: "In a cool atmosphere of shade trees and in the lovely setting of garden flowers at the home of Mrs. Ethel Smith of Perry street, the Barre Woman's club held a garden party yesterday afternoon. Despite the heat, the party was well-attended and those present declared themselves refreshed at the end of the afternoon. Tables of bridge were in play under the trees during the afternoon, and later delicious refreshments were served the guests. Mrs. Byron A. Wright and Mrs. L.R. Hutchinson poured. The executive board of the club was in charge of the garden party arrangements."

December 4, 1944: "Manager Earl Gibson of the Magnet theatre today announced that his theatre would sponsor, as it did in the fifth war loan drive, a children's war bond premiere in connection with the present war loan campaign. The premiere to be held at 10 o'clock Saturday morning, Dec. 9, will feature, 'The Texas Kid,' starring Johnny Mack Brown. This exciting picture will be supplemented by shorts and cartoons. Here's one way the kids of Barre can help their Uncle Sam with the war effort and, at the same time, be rewarded with a fine moving picture show. To gain admission children must buy or sell a war bond of any denomination.

Tickets to the premiere will be given at either of the two theatres or at any other bond-selling agency in the city."

January 8, 1945: "A well-attended meeting of the Brookside P.T.A. was held Friday evening. The organization voted to build and equip a school library in one of the small rooms and in the other plans to make a dispensary. After the meeting lunch was served by Mrs. Bainbridge and Mrs. McIver."

April 10, 1945: "A veritable stream of tin should be flowing along the streets of Barre this Sunday when Company E, Vermont state guard, collects tin cans for the war effort. John T. Nelson, local salvage committee chairman, met last night with Capt. Geno L. Guazzoni, company commander, and they decided to start the drive at 1 o'clock Sunday afternoon. Every ward in the city will be covered. Inasmuch as there has not been a tin can collection for months, householders should have a sizeable quantity ready for the company. Every householder is urged to place the cans on street curbs or piazzas where they may be easily picked up. Nelson stressed that only 'prepared' cans should be collected. To 'prepare' a can simply wash out the can, remove the labels, cut out both ends, flatten the can by stepping on it, and then place both ends inside the can. Uncle Sam needs that tin; will you give it to him?"

May 4, 1945: "Sgt. Frederick D. Piric, who has been spending a furlough with his wife and parents, Mr. and Mrs. Fred Pirie, of Tremont street, reported Monday to Fort Devens, Mass., for reassignment. He was to have rejoined his outfit in Italy, where he was wounded last winter, but with the surrender of the Germans there he has returned home for a ten-day furlough."

August 18, 1945: "A V-J day celebration was held at Carpenter's hall Wednesday by the employes of the local M.H. Fishman store. An entertainment program featured Miss Lucy Cano, accordion, accompanied by Miss Anita Cano, guitar. Group singing and dancing were in order. Morris Milkoff, manager of the store, addressed the group on post-war conditions and about their jobs in the future. One of the highlights was a victory march along Main street, led by Miss Cano playing her accordion. Refreshments were served by a committee consisting of Alba DeVecchi, Virginia Safford, Aracelia Cano and Esther Gallas."

Movie stars Ann Rutherford and Charles Laughton selling war bonds in Barre City Park, September 26, 1942. *Author's collection.*

October 5, 1945: "Mrs. John T. Watson has rejoined her husband in Barre where she will make her home now that she has been discharged from the army nurses corps at Fort Bragg, N.C., where she has been stationed since her 22 months' overseas service in England."

Chapter 5

After the War

1946–60

Although it was during this era that most Vermonters first laid eyes on a television, the day was not yet conceivable when the average American would set aside their newspaper in favor of less demanding sources of news. Still, at least one local newspaper, the *Montpelier Evening Argus*, was forced to suspend publication, on August 29, 1959, after being bought out by the *Times.* "Talk of the Town" briefly continued in the new *Times Argus*, but its last appearance was on June 2, 1960. One might speculate that someone had been confused that, while the newspaper ostensibly represented Barre and Montpelier equally, a column known as "Talk of the Town" was only about Barre. For whatever reason, however, the column's name was now "Barre News Notes":

January 3, 1946: "Police have reported a group of five or six youths of fourteen and fifteen years of age as having been apprehended for throwing stones or solid ice at passing vehicles on Maple avenue at about 8:45 o'clock on an evening earlier in the week. Before being taken into custody, the boys did succeed in breaking the left door window of a motorist from Washington, who with assistance from others, caught one of the pranksters and turned him over to police for questioning. The parents of the children were contacted, and arrangements made for payment of the damages to the broken glass."

February 8, 1946: "Seven members of the Women's Guild of the Episcopal church enjoyed a dinner party at the Venetian restaurant last evening. After the dinner the members adjourned to the home of Miss Iole Carusi of 16 Second street for a business meeting. Plans were made for a St. Patrick's tea and apron sale to take place in March."

May 3, 1946: "Although involving only the small sum of $2, a large sense of honesty was displayed by 11-year-old Diane Montague, daughter of Mr. and Mrs. Arthur E. Montague of 36 Park street yesterday. Returning home from her fifth grade studies at St. Monica's school, she found the mentioned money in the form of two bills folded together and lying on the sidewalk on Summer street. Continuing on home with her prize, she immediately asked her mother's permission to bring her find to the police station and make proper report of the incident. Police were grateful for the honesty shown by the young citizen who will be returned the money if the rightful owner does not offer to claim it."

July 8, 1946: "Chellis Collins, manager of Hooker's, is spending the week at Grand Rapids, Mich., and Chicago, visiting summer furniture markets."

November 16, 1946: "A small fire, believed to have started from a burning cigarette, caused damage to a chair and filled a second floor room with smoke at the Central Hotel about 2:30 o'clock this morning. Firemen were called and a pony extinguisher was used. A late retiring guest at the hotel is believed to have carelessly left the burning cigarette which ignited the upholstery."

December 5, 1946: "Christmas carols coming from the belfry of the Universalist church yesterday afternoon brought a Yuletide spirit to shoppers and others on the streets. The carols, issuing from two loudspeakers, were played over an electric record player. Yesterday afternoon was only a preliminary example of what the Christmas shoppers may expect during the last ten days of shopping. The equipment was installed under the sponsorship of the Barre Merchants' bureau."

June 5, 1947: "William Bisset, former Barre meat market proprietor who went to California more than a year ago, last week bought out a meat market at Whittier, where he makes his home with Mrs. Bisset and their daughter and son, Violet and David. He writes friends that the new meat market is a modern one with up-to-date equipment. Miss Bisset is employed by the Whittier National Trust and Savings bank."

A busy day during the Christmas shopping season in downtown Barre, late 1940s. *Aldrich Library Collection.*

July 9, 1947: "The Perry Real Estate agency has sold for Harry D. Holt and son the new house recently constructed by them on Tremont street to George M. and Willa B. Low of Wellesley, Mass., who purchase for a home and plan to take possession immediately."

August 6, 1947: "George Bennett of the East Barre road, proprietor of the Baltimore Lunch room, has purchased the 'Dog House,' a mobile hot dog and hamburger stand, from Charles Arnholm of Farwell street. The 'Dog House' makes trips daily throughout the business districts of the city, visiting business places, such as garages, stonesheds, filling stations and shops. The new proprietor will continue to follow the same route and call at the same places as the cart has been doing. Mr. Bennett will operate the cart himself and will sell hot dogs, hamburgers, coffee, ice cream, soda, cigarettes and chocolate bars."

September 6, 1947: "A. Russell White of 13 Second street, janitor at the city hall building, suffered a shoulder injury while working on the stage of the old Opera House yesterday afternoon. He was treated by Dr. William McFarland. Results of X-rays taken yesterday were awaited today to determine the full extent of the injury. Mrs. White reported this morning that he spent a restless night. While standing near a screen and staging a heavy weighted bag fell a distance of about 25 feet and struck him a glancing blow on the shoulder."

October 3, 1947: "Julian Martin, son of the Rev. and Mrs. Eldon H. Martin of French street, has been accepted into the a cappella choir at Ohio Wesleyan university."

January 6, 1948: "In court this morning Royal Potter, 36-year-old West Rutland trucking manager, pleaded guilty to a charge of speeding on the Barre-Williamstown road and was fined $10 and costs of $5.60. Halted yesterday by a member of the state police, Potter was charged in the warrant with having traveled at the speed of 70 miles per hour. He paid the fine and costs."

May 5, 1948: "One of the best brook trout reported locally this season was a 16½-inch fish landed yesterday by James Craddock, local pharmacist. The big brookie succumbed to the lure of a nightcrawler dangled in the stream near the Jackson farm on the South Barre-Williamstown road."

July 20, 1948: "Curtis R. Johnson, proprietor of the C.R. Johnson, Inc., Pontiac garage on the Montpelier road, recently acquired ownership of the Fairlee garage near the Orford turn and is operating it in conjunction with his local property. The garage was formerly Coffin's."

August 6, 1948: "Harley W. Kidder last evening addressed the union of employes of the capacitor division of the Rock of Ages corporation, at the regular monthly session of the union held in the Scampini block. He was introduced by the president of the union, Miss Elsie M. Williamson of 80 Hill street."

September 1, 1948: "Judge Arthur N. MacLeod of Graniteville, accompanied by Judge Norbert J. Towne of Northfield, left this morning for Rutland where they will attend a periodic conference of municipal judges. While in Rutland they will inspect the women's reformatory."

October 7, 1948: "Tom Davis of 25 Tremont street and David Miller of 167 Hill street returned this morning from Boston, where they attended the first game of the World Series yesterday."

November 19, 1948: "Miss Jennie Dunn, field secretary of the Katherine Gibb school in Boston, was an overnight guest Monday at the home of Mr. and Mrs. Robert Q. McDonnell of 61 Perry street. She addressed girls at Spaulding high school on Tuesday."

December 9, 1948: "Police collected $179.40 from the parking meters this morning, which represents the amount deposited by motorists in paying for parking time during the first three days of this week. The amount was reported to be one of the largest collected for the first three-day period of any period. Visiting Christmas shoppers are expected to swell the total collection for this week to well over $400."

January 5, 1949: "Moving of the Wesley R. Hoffman home at 385 North Main street from its location at the corner of North Main street and Maple avenue to a point some 100 feet further along the avenue was started yesterday by the H.A. Waugh Construction company. Excavation for the foundation and cellar at the proposed new location of the large building is being completed today. The house will be raised on steel fixtures then swung partly around and moved back so that it will be facing Maple avenue, closer to the property of Francis A. Cleary of 9 Maple avenue. Preparations for moving are expected to be completed within two weeks. The actual transportation of the building on huge rollers will be completed in about a month, H.A. Waugh stated. The present site of the Hoffman home will be converted into a filling station and garage which will be erected by Egidio J. Rulfo and John and Joseph Bossi, owners of the Twin City Gasoline company. Work on this project is expected to be started later this winter."

July 12, 1949: "William E. Reid of 76 Washington street, sales representative for the Dawson Macdonald company throughout the southern states, left yesterday for Boston, Mass., en route south to resume his employment, after visiting for several weeks at the home of his parents, Mr. and Mrs. Allan W. Reid."

August 19, 1949: "Co-Ad club members of the Congregational church will hold their corn roast this evening at 5:30 o'clock, at Windy Wood farm on Trow hill. The affair was postponed from last evening because of rain. All members are invited to attend."

September 6, 1949: "Valentino Acebo of River street is leaving today for Providence, R.I., where he will begin his first year at Bryant college."

November 4, 1949: "Carl Barteau has completed the building of his new home on the Barre-Montpelier road, and is now devoting his time to his radio business as well as managing the Aiken sporting goods store while Erwin Aiken is ill."

The Joshua Thwing mansion on North Main Street in North Barre, formerly known as "Thwingville." Photo probably taken in the 1940s. *Vermont Historical Society.*

December 9, 1949: "Miss Mary Barcomb of Beckley Court is to direct a nursery school, which will open January 2 and not a nursing school as was reported in yesterday's paper."

January 3, 1950: "Four New Year's day infants born Sunday at the Barre City hospital were a daughter at noon to Mr. and Mrs. Gaston Lafreniere of East Barre; a daughter at 1:15 p.m. to Mr. and Mrs. Dennis Lanctot of Graniteville; a son, Thomas James, at 3:27 p.m. to Mr. and Mrs. Clarence J. Fitzpatrick of Circle street; and a daughter at 5:50 p.m. to Mr. and Mrs. Aldrich of Lawrence avenue."

February 1, 1950: "A small but mighty group of barbershoppers from Barre, under the direction of Herbert D. Rusling of East Barre, presented a concert last night in Fairlee. This concert, which lasted about an hour and a half, consisted of chorus and quartet singing and A. Leroy Smith gave some humorous readings. Because of the poor road conditions the attendance at the concert was very small."

May 5, 1950: "After an absence of more than 40 years from her native homeland one of the older Italian residents of Barre, Mrs. Adele Monti of 264 North Main street, will embark from New York City aboard the steamship *Saturnia*, American Export lines, on May 18 for a three months visit in Italy. Mrs. Monti came to the United States in 1909 at the age of 30, residing in Batavia, N.Y., where she was occupied as a dressmaker. Two years later she married Salvador P. Monti in that city. The family later moved to Springfield and Chicago, Ill., and then to Clyde, Ohio, where Monti died in 1917. After the death of her husband she moved to Barre with her two children, Andrew and Lucia, and shortly thereafter Lucia died. Mrs. Monti has made her home in Barre since that time and became a naturalized citizen of the United States in 1925. At the age of 70 she is still enjoying good health and is looking forward to her trip with a great deal of enthusiasm. She will arrive at the port of Genoa about the first of June and from there she will go to Viggiu, Province of Varese, where she was born and spent her childhood. Other provinces in northern Italy are also included in her itinerary. Mrs. Monti's son, State Police Officer Andrew H. Monti, will accompany her to New York City from where she is to sail and will also meet her when she returns to the United States in August."

September 1, 1950: "Mrs. Peter Cano of Thurston place entertained the Barre Overseas Wives club last night. An employe of the Red Cross pharmacy, Mrs. Cano this week received her final American citizenship papers. She is the fourth member of the local club to have become an American citizen. Though she and Mr. Cano met in France, she was born in England and was a British subject."

November 3, 1950: "Postmaster Sergio Pasetto of Beckley street has been confined to his home for the past several days with a throat infection."

December 12, 1950: "Weekend visitors at the home of Mr. and Mrs. Armand Lafaille of Hill street were Mr. and Mrs. Leo Duquette of Fulford, P.W., Miss Maria Bourbonnais of Eastman, P.W., and Miss Madeleine Jolin of Montreal."

March 20, 1951: "William MacAllen of 26 Willey street has resumed his duties at the Barre Trust company after being confined to his home by illness for a couple weeks."

April 17, 1951: "Miss Marilyn McDonald of 47 Park street, daughter of Mr. and Mrs. Robert H. McDonald, has been pledged to Pi Beta Phi sorority, Massachusetts Alpha chapter, at Boston University College of Music. Miss McDonald, who is majoring in voice, is one of only four College of Music students ever pledged to this sorority. She sings in St. John's Episcopal church choir at Boston."

August 14, 1951: "Police have received complaints that youngsters are 'raiding' vegetable gardens and fruit trees in several sections of the city. One resident in the Prospect street section reported that much of her garden had been trampled and vegetables taken recently by young vandals. Police Chief Dennis Donahue issues a warning that parents should inform their youngsters against taking or destroying the property of others. Tomatoes and cucumbers are reported to be the particular choice of the garden pillagers."

September 11, 1951: "Corinne Bisson is among the 31 student nurses who enrolled yesterday at the Fanny Allen School of Nursing. The group will study anatomy and physiology, microbiology, chemistry, religion, psychology and sociology at St. Michael's college. The school year opened with a mass of the Holy Ghost in the Fanny Allen Chapel today."

October 5, 1951: "Mrs. Paul Greenwood of 18 Elm street is confined to her home because of a leg injury which she received Wednesday afternoon about three o'clock while shopping. As she reached the top of the stairs from the basement in the M.H. Fishman store, she allegedly tripped and fell forward, injuring her left knee and leg. She was taken to the hospital for X-rays and then returned to her home, where she is convalescing."

November 9, 1951: "The recreation department is sponsoring a teen age dance, tonight for all seventh and eighth graders from 6:45 to 8:50 p.m., to be held at the Barre City auditorium."

December 15, 1951: "Maj. Emmons Lombard of Church street, who is stationed at the army base in Boston, arrived in the city yesterday. He was accompanied by his daughter, Katherine, who will sing here in the 'Messiah' as a soloist tomorrow night. She is a Boston university senior. They will return to Boston late tomorrow night."

January 2, 1952: "Mayor Chauncey M. Willey was at his office in the Chamber of Commerce rooms today for the first time since suffering a broken shoulder bone in a fall at his home several weeks ago. He is expected to preside at the special city council meeting scheduled for the afternoon."

February 12, 1952: "Enio Cestaro, son of Mr. and Mrs. John Cestaro of 21 Berlin street, left yesterday for Fort Devens, Mass., where he will be examined for entrance into the army. Cestaro received his notice to appear a week ago and is due at Fort Devens today."

March 11, 1952: "Leo J. Cyr of 10 Liberty street left yesterday afternoon for Boston where he will attend a Montgomery Ward and Co., managers meeting. He will be gone for several days."

July 7, 1952: "Ralph M. Tobin of 23 Academy street, who was formerly employed with the Pratt-Whitney company at Hartford, Conn., has accepted employment as bartender at the Hotel Barre Cellar Grill."

August 4, 1952: "Mr. and Mrs. Alexander V. Acebo and daughter, Wendy Lee, left Saturday morning for a week's vacation with Mrs. Acebo's parents in Connecticut. Mr. Acebo will attend the graduation exercises at Bryant college on Aug. 8 where he will receive his bachelor of science degree."

December 11, 1952: "Miss Claire Rossi of 40 Ayers street was delightfully surprised last night upon entering the home of Mrs. Attilio Perantoni of 222 South Main street, to find 24 friends and relatives gathered to tender her a bridal shower in honor of her approaching marriage to Robert Lissor Saturday. The guest of honor received many lovely gifts and a social evening followed, during which, Mrs. Perantoni, who was in charge of the affair, served dainty refreshments."

February 6, 1953: "Earl W. Haggett of Montpelier pleaded guilty in Barre municipal court this morning to a meter violation charge on Jan. 26. Haggett paid a fine of $9.20. Haggett had parked his truck on North Main street between the hours of 9 a.m., and 6 p.m., on Jan. 26 without placing the necessary money in the meter. It was the first warrant issued in this city for such violations. Haggett was apprehended by the local police in front of City hall."

May 6, 1953: "In keeping with the custom of household spring cleaning, members of the fire department have been busy painting and otherwise improving their living quarters during the past few weeks. They report fewer interruptions to attend grass and brush fires this spring. The walls

Holy Name Parade, at North Main and South Seminary Streets, May 18, 1952. *Aldrich Library Collection.*

and ceilings of several upstairs rooms and hallways have been repainted, with varnish trimmings added."

August 7, 1953: "Alden LaMoy of 16 Oswald street, was honored last night at a stag party tendered by 50 friends and relatives at the Country House restaurant. He will marry Miss Clair Couture of East Barre Aug. 8, at St. Sylvester's church in Graniteville. Following a bountiful dinner, Kelman Craig, toastmaster, presented a purse of money in behalf of his friends and relatives. Arranging the party were Gerald Couture, Donald Bisson and Rawland LaMoy."

September 3, 1953: "The South End Garage has assumed the dealership for Austin automobiles, it was announced yesterday by Louis Pironi, proprietor. Pironi stated his business establishment will specialize in servicing automobiles of foreign make, such as the Austin, Hillman and M-G."

October 14, 1953: "Mr. and Mrs. Arthur C. Raeder of Portland, Me., are the parents of a son, Robert Douglas, born Thursday, October 8. The infant is the grandson of Mr. and Mrs. C.F.R. Bishop of 40 Eastern avenue."

November 13, 1953: "Mr. and Mrs. Ruperto Sierra of 81 Abbott avenue, have gone to St. Petersburg, Fla., for the winter months, and will return here next May. They left Barre by train on Sunday and have arrived at their destination."

December 14, 1953: "Levi Taft, former Barre resident, returned yesterday to New Haven, Conn., after spending two months with relatives here. Taft had remained longer than he intended, awaiting snow on which to do some hunting. Ironically the snow arrived the day after he left."

February 5, 1954: "The Barre fire department responded to a call at 7:05 last night to 13 Eastern avenue where a refrigerator motor was on fire. Extinguishers were used. The house is owned by Louis Garibaldi."

March 27, 1954: "Gusts of high velocity winds ripped down a sign, five feet by 12 feet, situated at the entrance of Arnholm's Motel on the Barre-Montpelier road, early Thursday morning. Arnholm stated that the sign had been placed in a cement foundation with four-inch pipe. Even thus seated the sign was flattened to the ground. Arnholm also stated he had seen many other signs, along the highway which had been blown down by the fierce windstorm."

June 18, 1954: "Single blasts on the fire horn heard yesterday and this morning were attributed by Fire Chief Roy MacDonald to a defective fuse. All lines in the alarm system were checked he said, and one fuse at the fire station is believed to have caused the trouble. Passing trucks may have set up a vibration which touched off the sensitive alarm, he said."

August 13, 1954: "Lawrence Chouinard has resumed his duties at Bennett's garage after a vacation."

September 17, 1954: "The single house with garage located at 84 Batchelder street and owned by Mr. and Mrs. Stanley Jacobs has been sold to Mr. and Mrs. Elmer Strobridge of this city. The purchasers acquired the property for a home. The sale was made by Howard W. Geake, real estate agent."

November 19, 1954: "Seventy-five per cent of the city was without electric power for a short while late yesterday afternoon after a 33,000-

volt insulator failed in the Granite street sub power station. The customers affected were those who get their power from this station. The company went on emergency line shortly after the failure."

December 13, 1954: "The Lincoln-Ayers street P.T.A. will hold its December meeting tonight at the Lincoln school auditorium. Sgt. Richard Curtis of the Vermont state police will show a film and speak on the subject, 'Safety Comes First.' Refreshments will follow the program."

May 18, 1955: "A comely Barre area young lady was a near winner in the regional contest sponsored by the National Press Photographers' Association over the week end. Miss Ann Bowen, 19-year-old daughter of Mr. and Mrs. A. Wynn Bowen of Hill street extension, reached the semi-finals in the beauty parade which highlighted the Sunday afternoon session of the photographers convention. The session was held at the Eastern States Exposition grounds near Springfield, Mass. Miss Bowen, clerk in the office of the State Fish and Game department of Montpelier, was the only Vermont entry. She was selected through the Vermont Development Commission and was 'sponsored' in the beauty contest by Kenneth Campbell, photographer for the *Brattleboro Reformer* newspaper. Winner of the contest and a trip to Colorado was Miss Beverly Jansen of Providence, R.I. Miss Bowen reported having an enjoyable week end, even though she had not had time for detailed preparations."

June 8, 1955: "Robert Cecchini of 27 Maple avenue, sophomore at the University of Maine, Orono, Me., will arrive home today after the completion of his final examination."

January 3, 1956: "Mrs. Martha Jurras of 3 Bemis place left last week for Old Greenwich, Conn., where she will spend the winter months with her son and daughter-in-law, Mr. and Mrs. John Jurras. The latter two visited for a few days last week with relatives in Barre and vicinity."

February 9, 1956: "A 1,000 watt floodlight was installed yesterday at the Granite City Ski Bowl and a large number of high school and grammar school students as well as a good number of adults, enjoyed the well-lighted slopes until 10 o'clock. Comments were heard that it was like skiing in the daytime."

March 10, 1956: "In the celebration of the Girl Scout birthday Monday, the scouts and leaders of Troop 2 will present a one-half hour program over radio station WSKI at 10:15 a.m., on 'Looking

New housing on Trow Hill in Barre Town, late 1950s. *Vermont Historical Society.*

About' program. Included in the program will be a short skit, 'The Hour of Decision.'"

June 15, 1956: "The police department reported today that the department does not tolerate or register magazine salesmen who regularly appear in town at this time of the year. A city ordinance exists which prohibits such practices and calls for a fine if apprehended."

December 10, 1956: "Erardo Cardini, a granite sculptor, left Friday to return to Baveno, Italy, after spending several months here working at Consolidated Memorials and visiting with his sister, Mrs. A. Pacetti of 38 Railroad street. He sailed on the *Christopher Columbus*. Cardini plans to return to Barre next spring when he will bring his family with him."

January 9, 1957: "An alarm from box 71 brought the fire department to Consolidated Memorials Granite company this morning at 1:25. The alarm was sounded by a faulty sprinkler and there was no fire. The department shut off and drained the system and called the foreman of the plant. The all-out was sounded seven minutes later."

March 19, 1957: "Harry Lipman of Miami, Fla., arrived in the city last night for a two-day business visit."

April 10, 1957: "The renovation project at the old Magnet theatre is proceeding at a good pace. The H.A. Waugh construction company is doing the work. The entire interior has been torn out and the side doors on Pearl street blocked up. The front of the building has been torn out and a barricade erected on the sidewalk. A center partition has been put in place showing that there will be considerable space for two stores when the work is completed."

August 8, 1957: "Mr. and Mrs. Wendell Fitts and children have returned to their home on Maple Grove street after spending a vacation at Moody Beach, Me."

September 3, 1957: "Stephen Martin, son of the Rev. Dr. and Mrs. Eldon H. Martin of French street, has returned to Washington, D.C., to resume his studies at George Washington School of Law. He has spent the summer as a clerk in the law office of Finn and Davis."

December 13, 1957: "The Skyline Pomalift and rope tow will operate on a limited basis starting this Saturday and Sunday from 1 to 4 p.m. After a good snow base is established, regular lift hours will be announced. The snow base must be secure and the lighting system completed before fulltime operation."

January 8, 1958: "The Recreation Department has plans for the girls in the second grade of the public and parochial schools. There has been such interest shown in the third grade baton twirling class by so many youngsters in the second grade that a new such class is being organized. Instruction which will be given by Miss Nancy Cornish assisted by Miss Lynn Drown will begin today at 3:45 in the basement of the auditorium."

May 13, 1958: "The brick building located at 48 Granite St., and formerly the site of several Italian bakeries in years past, has been sold to the Rock of Ages Corp. This property, together with a right-of-way to Granite St., was owned by the Washington Fruit Co. Arrangements for this sale were made by Charles J. Zanleoni, realtor."

October 8, 1958: "Andrew Monti of 44 Berkeley St. returned to Barre last night by air from New York City. While there he attended three of the World Series games, Saturday, Sunday and Monday."

November 14, 1958: "Robert Slora, 11 year old son of Mr. and Mrs. James Slora of Pine Hill Road, shot his first deer in Groton, while hunting with his father. It had 8 points and weighed 170 lbs."

December 16, 1958: "Two sets of the Granite Center Square Dance Club met Sunday at the home of Mr. and Mrs. Dean Blanchard, East Barre for a Christmas party. After the dinner, prepared by Mrs. Blanchard, a social hour was enjoyed during which gifts were exchanged."

January 7, 1959: "Films on free enterprise and the oil industry were shown to members of the Everyman Club of the First Presbyterian Church last night by a representative of the Tydol Oil Co. The club president, Dr. Ralph Caccavo, conducted the meeting during which a nominating committee was named to present a report at the next meeting. The supper which preceded the meeting was prepared by William Watt and Neil Shannon."

February 13, 1959: "Ritual chapter night was observed last evening at the meeting of the Women of the Moose. Mrs. Gertrude Murray was in charge of activities. During the meeting which was held in the Moose Hall, the charter was draped in memory of the late Viola Bailey who died on Jan. 28. Two new members were initiated during the session last night."

August 29, 1959: "The new five-room ranch style home, recently constructed by LaGue Inc., and located on Crescent St., has been purchased by Dante and June Caranchini of South Royalton."

August 31, 1959: "James Howard of South Barre and Gerard and Janice Foster, 10 Hillside Ave., Barre, left Saturday for Ferry Beach, Maine where they will attend the Youth Laboratory of Liberal Religious Youth. The week-long conference is held at the summer conference grounds of the Universalist Church of America. The three, who represent the youth group of the Barre Universalist Church, were joined yesterday by Whitney Maxfield of 44 Brook St., Barre."

September 18, 1959: "Mrs. Joann Wobby announced this morning that the Heiress Motel at 573 North Main St., Barre, has completed installation of telephones in the rooms. This, she reported, is the first motel in the Barre area to have phones for patrons."

November 3, 1959: "Seven members of the Santa's Workshop Bazaar committee on decorations met last night at the home of Mrs. Bernard Chenette, in Barre. Decoration projects are progressing and next week's committee project will concentrate on the fashioning of wreaths. The Catholic Daughters of America sponsored bazaar will be held Saturday, Dec. 5."

Aerial view of downtown Barre, circa 1960. The street to the left is Summer Street; to the right, North Main Street. *Aldrich Library Collection.*

January 9, 1960: "Storytellers for this morning's 'Story Hour' at Aldrich Public Library were members of Barre Girl Scout troops and students at Vermont College in Montpelier. The weekly sessions are offered children in grades 1 through 4, under the sponsorship of the Barre Woman's Club."

May 5, 1960: "Robert Sanguinetti received his varsity letter in skiing at a recent letter awards presentation at Tufts College in Medford, Mass. He is the son of Mr. and Mrs. Leo Sanguinetti of 59 Currier St., Barre."

June 2, 1960: "B. John Shadroui of South Barre has completed his sophomore year at the Parsons School of Design in New York City and is home for the summer. He returned with his father, John B. Shadroui, his brother, Robert, and uncle, Tony Shadroui, of Barre."

Chapter 6

Slow Fade-Out

1960–70

By the time "Barre News Notes" arrived on the scene, "Talk of the Town" was a shell of its former self. Almost all of the items now fell into one of a few categories: club news, minor crimes, comings and goings, school news, church news, wedding and baby showers and minor traffic accidents. Probably the only type of item to be added to the mix was the real estate notice. This was a great American era of suburbia and homeownership. As Barre City had mostly run out of room for more houses, a great many homes (many with the word "ranch" in their descriptions) were being built in Barre Town. The real estate item in "Barre News Notes" served a dual purpose: to indicate that the buyer was moving up in the world and to provide advertisement for the real estate agent, who was invariably named at the end of the item.

A sampling follows:

June 3, 1960: "Mrs. Paul MacDuff of Trow Hill was honored at a stork shower Wednesday night at the home of Mrs. Eugene Bilodeau, Sheridan St., Barre. About 20 were present. Mrs. MacDuff was presented a corsage and miscellaneous gifts. Refreshments, including a decorated cake, were served. In charge of arrangements were Mrs. Bilodeau, Mrs. Robert Waugh and Miss Sandra Laquerre."

October 5, 1960: "Women's night at the Barre Auditorium has been set on Monday nights at 8–10 p.m. Approximately 10 attended a preliminary meeting last night to form plans for the winter season. In the event the building is in use on that night, the events will be held downstairs in the Thompson Memorial Building."

November 14, 1960: "Fourteen members of the Lighthouse, Barre's teen center, appeared on WCAX-TV Saturday night on the 'Dance Date' program. They were Carole Pryor, David Corliss, Alan Cumming, Jacqueline Gray, Roberta Paige, Jackie Jacques, Susan Lunt, Charles Griffin, Catherine MacEnany, John McLeod, Brenda Watson, Douglas Bassett, Karen Gignac and Ronald Gover. Mr. and Mrs. Maurice Gignac of 96 Maple Ave., were chaperones. Station officials guided the young people about the studio and toured the control area of the station."

January 2, 1961: "Booth R. Martin, son of Mr. and Mrs. A.R. Martin, 16 Delmont Ave., Barre, was recently initiated into Alpha Delta Sigma fraternity at Babson Institute in Wellesley, Mass. Martin is a senior at Babson."

May 26, 1961: "Approximately 50 Girl Scouts and Brownies from Barre drilled last night at Currier Park for tomorrow's VFW parade in Montpelier. Peter Giacherio led the girls in the technique of marching. The banner which the girls will use in the parade was made by Gordon Lane and will be carried by Bianca Billings and Paula Guiduli, members of the newly-formed Senior Troop 4. The leader marching with them will be Mrs. Ruth Donahue, Troop 16."

June 5, 1961: "Mrs. Angelo Bardelli and two children, Anna and Eugenio, 1 Bank St., Barre, left by plane last night from Boston to spend the summer visiting relatives in Italy."

October 18, 1961: "In observance of National Newspaper Week, the Aldrich Public Library has on exhibit a number of early copies of Barre newspapers. They include flood editions of an earlier *Barre Times* (a weekly paper) and of the *Barre Herald*, a century or more ago."

November 9, 1961: "Skyline Ski Area officials have announced that a ski school will be available seven days a week and four nights a week. David Friberg will be the instructor. A ski club is also planned for the winter, with dates of meetings to be announced soon."

January 2, 1962: "Mr. and Mrs. Harry Lipman, Windy Wood Road, Barre, left Sunday for a two-week vacation at St. Thomas, Virgin Islands. Lipman is proprietor of Harry's Discount Store on the Barre-Montpelier Road."

February 12, 1962: "Mr. and Mrs. Lucien Rivard, 8 Hall St., and Mr. and Mrs. Raoul Maurice, 262 Prospect st., Barre spent the weekend in Montreal where they attended the Ice Follies."

March 10, 1962: "The Rev. and Mrs. Ernest L. Seely and son, Michael, of 48 Perry St., Barre, are in North Berwick, Maine, having been called by the sudden death Thursday of his mother, Mrs. J.L. Seely. Funeral services will be held in the Maine community on Monday. The Rev. Yorke Peeler Jr. of Barre will serve the pulpit of the Barre Congregational Church tomorrow in the absence of the Rev. Mr. Seely."

November 28, 1962: "Miss Jill Ann Blaise of Keeseville, N.Y., spent Thanksgiving vacation with her uncle and aunt, Mr. and Mrs. Stanley Blaise, 29 Brook St., Barre."

December 8, 1962: "A combined business meeting and stag party took place Thursday night at the Howard Johnson restaurant on the Barre-Montpelier Road. Members of the Penn State Life Insurance Co. office attended and honored Donald Murray on his forthcoming marriage. He will wed Miss Carmen Carcoba of Barre."

January 4, 1963: "Edward Perantoni has returned to his junior year studies at Maryville College, Maryville, Tenn., after spending the holiday recess with his parents, Mr. and Mrs. Olvero Perantoni, 10 Murray St., Barre."

February 15, 1963: "A. Fracassi, proprietor of Fric's Restaurant, N. Main Street, Barre, is celebrating his 34th business anniversary today. He opened the eating spot Feb. 15, 1929, and it is still in operation in the same location."

May 4, 1963: "Mr. and Mrs. Robert Sierra, proprietors of Bebe's Restaurant in the Vermont Shopping Center, have returned from the New England Hotel and Restaurant Show in Boston, held April 30, May 1 and 2."

June 4, 1963: "Mrs. Clarissa Nutbrown, S. Main Street, Barre, returned to her duties in the boys' clothing department at Montgomery Ward's today after a week's illness."

November 22, 1963: "Wilfred Fisher of Barre, district deputy grand exalted ruler, Vermont North, will make his official visitation to the Montpelier Elks Lodge tomorrow afternoon. He will be accompanied by a large number of Barre Elks who will attend the initiation of a class of candidates and participate in an evening program."

January 11, 1964: "Francis Putney of Graniteville, who fractured a wrist this week while working on the emergency Civil Defense water supply system in Graniteville, is recuperating at home, according to a member of his family. His condition remains about the same. He is under medical attention. The Putney family was pleased Thursday to have Gov. Philip H. Hoff and Commissioner William H. Baumann visit them. The governor had expressed a desire to visit Putney after he heard of his injuries received while at work on the emergency pumping station."

February 14, 1964: "The ABH Home Demonstration Club met with Mrs. Richard Davis, 11 Bolster Ave., Barre, last night. A new member, Mrs. Robert Guinn of Abbott Avenue, was introduced. A suggested revision of the by-laws was discussed by Mrs. Donald Smith. A vote will be taken at a later meeting. The topic, 'Leftovers,' was in charge of Mrs. Leonard Norkeveck and Mrs. James Martin. They suggested appetizing uses of leftover food and served samples. A Chinese auction and refreshments concluded the meeting. Mrs. Gordon Lynds, Camp Street, will be hostess for the March 11 meeting when Mrs. Hazel Brown will speak on 'Cash and Credit.'"

October 16, 1964: "Barre police reported this morning that five youngsters who were pulling a home-made mannequin in front of moving cars at Wellington and Merchant Sts., causing considerable consternation to motorists, have been reported to their parents. Police Chief Floyd Chandler said there will be no juvenile petitions asked for in the cases. The ringleader of the youths, Chandler said, got a sound seat warming from his father—and that closed the issue."

February 11, 1965: "The Chicago Club met last night with Mrs. Roland Trott, 300 Tremont St., Barre. A Maine lobster dinner was served with Kentucky coffee, with a social evening following."

March 8, 1965: "R. Stillman Bosworth of Plainfield terminated his employment Saturday at the Granite City Creamery where he had been working for the past seven years. He has been employed by the IBM firm at its Essex Junction plant and started working there today."

April 5, 1965: "Judith Watson of 21 Delmont Ave., Barre, was named to the dean's list for outstanding scholastic work in the term just ended at the Rochester Business Institute. She is a graduate of

Spaulding High School and is enrolled in business administration and data processing course."

July 16, 1965: "Mr. and Mrs. George Thompson and daughter Christie of Ottawa, Ont., who have been visiting Mrs. Bathia Paterson of 158 Washington St., Barre, have left for Nova Scotia. They are traveling by trailer."

November 15, 1965: "Saturday afternoon 10 schoolmates of Stanley Sabens had dinner at the Country House to help him celebrate his 10th birthday. Following the opening of gifts the group went to Twin City Lanes. Stanley is the son of Mr. and Mrs. Stanley Sabens of the Barre-Montpelier Road."

December 13, 1965: "Barre firemen were called to N. Main St. Sunday to wash down gas leaking from a 1961 sedan. The alarm was called into the station at 2:25 p.m. from the Moose Club. The gas was washed down a nearby drain with a booster line."

March 25, 1966: "Mr. and Mrs. Gordon E. Akley and daughter Patricia of 4 Cliff St., Barre, leave today for Boston where they will meet their older daughter, Nancy, a student at Simmons College, and continue to Falmouth, Mass., to attend the New England Music Festival concert. Their son, Norman, is a member of the Spaulding delegation at the festival. Nancy will return with them to Barre for her spring vacation period."

July 6, 1966: "The family of Vico F. Masi of 94 Beckley Street is vacationing in Woodsville, N.H., at the home of Mrs. Masi's mother, and will remain until July 30."

October 7, 1966: "Area residents Thursday night had a clear view of two satellites as they lurched across the sky. Echo 11 appeared at approximately 8:08 p.m. 14 degrees above the eastern horizon, moving south to north, right on schedule. Shortly afterward, Pageos showed up on time 50 degrees above the northeast horizon, traveling from southeast to northwest. Pageos was due seven minutes after Echo 11. Both satellites made later passages above this viewing area, but in different paths, Echo 11 at 9:57 and Pageos at 11:19 p.m.

December 6, 1966: "The Can-do 4-H Club held a meeting last week at the home of Mrs. Quincy Perry, Woodland Drive. Officers elected were president, Becky Perry; secretary, Melissa Bedia; vice president,

Patty Duff; treasurer, Ellen Perry; news reporter, Cindy Gomez; project leader, Kathy Zagroba; singing and cheerleader, Susan Churchill; game leader, Nancy Houle and help leader, Patty Wilde. The next meeting will be held Dec. 13, when the Christmas party will be held."

June 20, 1967: "Mrs. Katherine H. Kerr of Pine Hill Road in Barre, an eighth grade math teacher at Spaulding Graded School, is the recipient of a National Science Foundation Award for teachers of math at the junior high school level. Mrs. Kerr will be attending the Summer Institute of Math at the Colgate University in Hamilton, N.Y. from June 25 to Aug. 6."

August 28, 1967: "Area motorists experienced some difficult driving conditions late yesterday afternoon—not from road conditions but from bugs. Millions of tiny winged insects filled the air in this vicinity and for several miles south and east. They piled up on car windshields in such volume that visibility was affected and drivers had to stop for cleanup jobs."

September 22, 1967: "Mr. and Mrs. Richard Cotnoir, of 7 Sunrise Ave., attended the annual meeting of the Vermont Petroleum Association at Basin Harbor yesterday. Mr. Cotnoir won an award in the service station of the year contest. He is the proprietor of Dick's Chevron Station, S. Main Street."

January 5, 1968: "Miss Gail Bagalio of Websterville returned by plane yesterday to the Ringling School of Art in Sarasota, Fla., after spending the holiday period with her parents, Mr. and Mrs. Lincoln Bagalio."

March 20, 1968: "'Historical Buildings in Vermont' will be the topic of Robert Burley on Thursday at 7:45 p.m. before the members of the American Association of University Women. They will meet at the home of Mrs. Alban Richey, 194 Washington St., Barre."

August 26, 1968: "Douglas J. Cooke has been transferred from the Heaton Hospital in Montpelier to the Central Vermont Hospital. His wife, Jacqueline, is also at the Central Vermont Hospital." [Central Vermont Hospital had just opened for business that same month.]

September 9, 1968: "The first fall meeting of the Parent-Teacher Organization of St. Monica's Parish will be held tonight at 8 at St. Monica's School. The teachers will explain to parents in two sessions the program of the particular grade in each subject and what will be expected of the students as far as home work and other activities are concerned. Dues will be payable and refreshments will be served."

October 4, 1968: "Mrs. S.P. Hatch of 14 Terrace Ave., Barre, reports a bloom and a bud on an Easter Lily she cut back and saved for later planting. Mrs. Hatch also says her poinsettia is doing well, which she cut back at Christmas time and planted."

February 6, 1969: "On Feb. 12 at 1:30 p.m. William N. Emery, the executive director of the Barre Public Housing Authority, will speak on the progress of the turn-key project at the Hotel Barre at a meeting at the senior Citizens Center, 79 N. Main St., Barre. He will also give information and assistance in filing applications for a unit in the public low-rent general housing project on Allen Street. This project is also under the jurisdiction of the Barre PHA. Inquiries on this program may be made at the Center."

April 7, 1969: "The Women's Fellowship of the Barre Congregational Church will meet at 9:30 a.m. Wednesday, April 9, at the church. Coffee will be served followed by the program, 'Pat's Poetry.' Co-chairmen of arrangements are Mrs. Arthur Hill Jr. and Mrs. Paul McLaughlin."

June 11, 1969: "Barre Public Housing Authority Executive-Director William Emery began moving his family to a new home in the Town of Washington today. The Emerys had been utilizing the living quarters adjoining the BPHA offices at 30 Washington St."

December 17, 1969: "Buttura and Sons Inc., Barre granite manufacturers, has been notified that the film footage shot by a CBS camera crew about two months ago, will be telecast on the *Sixty Minutes* show during February. It is expected announcement of the actual date will be made later. The crew was here with Harry Reasoner as narrator to take pictures of the various manufacturing operations in the plant. A visit was also made to the quarries for the pictures, showing the beginning of the process of creating a granite memorial."

February 12, 1970: "The public in Barre has an opportunity to view the 'moon rocks' brought back by the crew of Apollo 11 today and Friday. The display will be in the corner window of the Peoples National Bank of Barre during those days. It has been made available through Gov. Deane C. Davis and has been on display at the Sprague Electric Co. plant in Barre, the Barre Town Elementary School and all Barre City schools."

J.J. Newberry's five-and-dime store, circa 1975. *Aldrich Library Collection.*

March 19, 1970: "Steven Ironside and Wayne Lafountain of the Barre DeMolay yesterday washed the windows at the Senior Citizens Activity Center as their contribution to DeMolay Week activities. The youths were assisted by Ed Brault, a member of the Senior Citizens Club."

April 7, 1970: "Mrs. Ginger Owen received a telephone call Friday morning from her son, Sgt. Darell Owen, who is with the U.S. Army serving in Vietnam. She said that she could hear him very clearly."

June 26, 1970: "Bradley Scott and Chauncey Liese of East Barre, Kevin Hurley of Trow Hill and Dwight Coffrin of Currier Street are among the Spaulding graduates now at Johnson State College attending orientation sessions."

September 19, 1970: "Miss Maureen Sumner of 96 Washington St., Barre, a June graduate of Spaulding High School, leaves Sunday, Sept. 20, to enroll at Champlain College, Burlington."

December 15, 1970: "Barre City firefighters were called at 5:40 p.m., Monday to 70 Prospect St., to a three-story wooden house, owned by Mary Romanos, where a faulty blower switch burned out the gas heater blower. No equipment was used by the firemen and the switch was replaced. The fire occurred in an apartment occupied by Mrs. Elwin Blood. Engine 2 and three men responded."

Afterword

I'm sorry. You don't know these people. This means nothing to you.
—Neil Young, liner notes, Tonight's the Night *(1975)*

The final years of "Barre News Notes" bore little resemblance to the old "Talk of the Town" of the early twentieth century. Gone was any humor or quirkiness, and in addition, there were much fewer items. It did, nonetheless, continue to serve its function of keeping readers informed. Probably sometime in the mid- to late 1980s, the last "Barre News Notes" column was published. It had, for several years, consisted solely of club news items that somehow didn't seem to fit anywhere else.

In the mid-1990s, the *Times Argus* revived "Talk of the Town" as a twice-weekly column, which was still being published in 2011. This seemed to be inspired by the humorous items from the column's early years, telling of offbeat events or providing local promotional news, all in a quirky, engaging style. Conspicuously missing were any routine "comings and goings" items or anything else that might be considered as of interest only to those who were acquainted with the people being discussed.

The late George Gladding, who worked in management at the *Times Argus*, once told me that the local column was axed because people were getting their houses broken into when criminals would read in "Barre News Notes" that they would be out of town for a week on vacation. However, it would seem as if this was not only a reason *for*—but also a symptom *of*—the slow demise of the local column in general.

The title "Talk of the Town" is something of a misnomer. It implies a gossipy quality that the column did not actually possess (although the "Barre Bundle" had it to some degree). When the seventeen-year-old Miller girl is hustled off to her "aunt's" for a few months, when Mr. Edwards has been seen frequenting the saloons a little too regularly, when there seems to be something wrong with the Robinson boy because he's never been married and still lives with his mother—speculation on people and situations similar to this can be considered "gossip." The closest "Talk of the Town" came to this was when it would duly report on the police arresting a named individual for any petty or not-so-petty crime. (I have, in fact, refrained from providing any samples in this book of the latter type of item, because I don't want to embarrass anyone still living or their descendants, and because I still live here.)

That said, I think that the impulse to butt into (or at least know of) the business of others was the primary motivation to create a column like "Talk of the Town." Gossip, for all its destructive qualities, is not found outside of close-knit communities where people look after each other, if a little too zealously. The small-town busybodies so reviled in Sinclair Lewis's 1925 novel *Main Street*, for example, were closed minded while also having an intense interest in their neighbors. Lewis was not wrong to mock this, but something is lost if we lose interest altogether in things going on around us that don't directly affect us.

If I may say something to outdate this book more quickly, the social networking website, while not a perfect replacement for face-to-face contact with one's neighbors, at least gives one more immediate access to those in the community who are connected to oneself, providing news of their activities and thoughts that would otherwise go unnoticed. This, to some degree, is why columns like "Talk of the Town" existed: to provide a quick, easy-to-scan page that would keep readers informed about local doings.

About the Author

Russell Belding loves the smell of old books in the morning, or any other time of the day for that matter. His house is filled with more books than he will ever be able to read. When he was a teenager, he traveled by bicycle to every township in Vermont. He has been coasting on that achievement ever since. He graduated in 1990 from Norwich University's Adult Degree Program under the tutelage of local legend Dick Hathaway. He has been researching the minutiae of Barre history for twenty years. He has been employed by the State of Vermont for nearly thirty years. He has a vast collection of pop music on various formats and can spot the anachronism in just about any TV show or movie that is set in the past, usually by virtue of the wrong song playing in the background. Aside from that, he doesn't consider himself to be too annoying. He lives in Barre with his wife, Lori, their two dogs and their cat. This is his third book.